MW01054783

WE'RE
ALL
IN THIS
TOGETHER...

ALSO BY TOM PAPA

You're Doing Great!: And Other Reasons to Stay Alive

Your Dad Stole My Rake: And Other Family Dilemmas

WE'RE ALL IN THIS TOGETHER...

SO MAKE SOME ROOM

Tom Papa

ST. MARTIN'S
PRESS
NEW YORK

First published in the United States by St. Martin's Press,
an imprint of St. Martin's Publishing Group

Printed in the United States of America. For information, address St. Martin's Publishing Group, 120 Broadway, New York, NY 10271.

www.stmartins.com

Designed by Steven Seighman

Library of Congress Cataloging-in-Publication Data is available upon request.

ISBN 978-1-250-28009-1 (hardcover)
ISBN 978-1-250-28010-7 (ebook)

Our books may be purchased in bulk for promotional, educational, or business use. Please contact your local bookseller or the Macmillan Corporate and Premium Sales Department at 1-800-221-7945, extension 5442, or by email at MacmillanSpecialMarkets@macmillan.com.

First Edition: 2023

10 9 8 7 6 5 4 3 2

For Tom and Elaine

CONTENTS

INTRODUCTION

I still get the old-timey newspaper delivered. Every morning I walk out, wave to my neighbors, pick up the paper and proudly bring it inside. But lately I've just been tossing it in a pile with the other unopened newspapers. Sometimes I'm just not in the mood for a scary movie.

When I'm in this state it's comforting to slow down and look to the past in order to realize that I'm not alone. We belong to something greater—an ongoing story that has been written throughout time and has now been handed off to us. Whether we like it or not, we're all in this together.

No single person made the world we live in. There wasn't one guy or gal who invented the computer, the Styrofoam cooler or that elastic band that holds your underwear up. Zillions of little decisions made by millions of little minds have unknowingly worked together to create this complex and fantastic world. It's nice to know that while I'm working on perfecting my olive bread there are people out there helping us to live healthier lives, fighting injustice and coming up with new flavors of soft serve ice cream.

Thankfully, people have been succeeding and screwing up for centuries, leaving us an ancient treasure map full of experiences, directions and clues that can help guide us along. If we can just pay attention and avoid the quicksand, sea monsters and murderous pirates, we'll be okay.

Humans have figured out how to eat, how to sleep and how to cheat on their taxes for years. Whatever question you have, someone has asked it before you. How am I going to eat this Oreo? How often should I floss? What happens when one of the kids flushes a pile of Legos down the toilet?

And the bigger questions: Can I live with someone who isn't a good kisser? How do I explain to my dog that I'm seeing other people? Is it normal to have fantasies about leaving my family and joining a mariachi band? These problems have all been faced before.

Sure, we're all unique and you are special, you little you, but on the other hand, we're all pretty much the same. We all eventually start to walk and talk and pick out ill-fitting shirts and get bad haircuts. We make mistakes, trip over nothing and proudly enter a party without realizing our fly is open, and that's okay.

We also made smartphones and cars. We made stuffed-crust pizza, churros and cannoli. We made zippers that work and Velcro that works even better. We made plastic, deodorant and bubble gum. And the really smart ones are improving medicine, saving lives and hopefully will figure out the global thermostat and lower the temperature a bit.

We collectively move forward while deciding what's worth

keeping. Luggage with wheels? We'll keep it. Selfie sticks? No, thank you. And where have all the electric can openers gone? There was a time when they were on every counter; now it's been decided, without a single meeting, that the handheld works just fine and the counter space should be used for the latest air fryer they say we can't live without.

But as incredible as we are, there are also primitive instincts in all of us that, if gone unchecked, threaten to slow all the progress we've made. Yes, we invented flight and airplanes and an intricate airline system that transports human beings safely around the globe. We did all of that, but we are also capable of jumping out of our seats, hiking up our denim board shorts and making a run for the emergency exit at thirty thousand feet.

The current disconnect and discontentment that many people are feeling out there are very real, causing full-grown adults to lash out in the aisles of Target like toddlers who are overwhelmed by the world around them. As institutions change, human rights are challenged or taken away, and digital isolation cuts us off from one another, we need to find new ways to connect.

I know that connecting with your fellow man can be uncomfortable. Locking eyes with a stranger on a crowded shuttle bus—or even worse, when you are the only two on the shuttle bus—can be pretty weird, but it's important.

We truly need one another, and all have our part to play. And just in case anyone reading this is responsible for improving soft serve ice cream, let me just say that I'm a fan of your chocolate-and-vanilla swirl, but I often wonder what it would taste like with just a hint of sourdough. Somebody must have given it a try and if not, hopefully, you'll get on that.

YOU'RE NOT TOTALLY CRAZY

....

From the minute I laced up my Converse All Stars and walked out of the comfort of my childhood home and into Miss Conway's kindergarten class, I was keenly aware that I was different. This wasn't good.

Suddenly, the orange corduroy pants I wore, the stuff my mom made for lunch and the dances I did so proudly at home were called out, mocked and turned into nicknames that I never asked for. I didn't want to be known as Tommy Salami. I wanted to blend in and be normal. I still do.

But as my grandmother would say while she fished a paper towel out of her bra to pat down her sweaty forehead, "There's no such thing as normal. Everybody's a mess."

Nana was kind of right. It's true that we're all a bit of a disaster, but I would argue that's precisely what makes us normal. Despite what the schoolyard bullies may have attacked you for, all our odd and quirky behaviors are universal.

So when you get dressed for work and reach into the pockets of what you thought was a clean pair of pants and you find a mix of dog treats, rubber bands and Hershey's Kiss wrappers, don't assume that you can't wear those pants. Sure, it's obvious they've already been worn, and you may not even have a dog, but how often do pants need to be washed, anyway? If you can't smell them from across the room, throw on your shoes, fix your hair and get going. Everybody does this; you're totally normal.

It's also normal to see a good friend of yours on the street, stop, turn and run the other way. This may be someone you love. You've been to their home. You've celebrated holidays together. And now you're ducked behind a mailbox, just praying they don't see you as they pass by. Well, don't feel bad about what you did, because I promise you, they've walked away from you too. That's what friends do.

They see you coming at the farmers market and quickly hide behind a bunch of plantains. Does this mean they prefer the company of a strange banana to you? No, they just couldn't deal with you and all your stuff at that moment. Neither of you are selfish or antisocial, you're just people with issues and complicated faces and what you did was normal.

Being a person means that you contain a certain amount of rude self-interest that needs to be balanced with the interests of others, and sometimes they lose. I'd love to say that I constantly help everyone around me and put their interests first, but that's simply not true. I'd like to be the guy who brings in the neighbor's garbage cans or helps set up for the school play, but I'm not even that helpful to the family I live with.

I never stir the oil into a new jar of peanut butter. My family wants that all-natural stuff that comes with two inches of oil on top and requires a half hour of intense stirring that results in a greasy, slimy mess on me, the knife and the sides of the jar. Fine, I'll buy it, but I'm not stirring it.

"What is wrong with you? It's your turn," my wife will say.

"It can't be my turn, because I'm not playing that game."

"What game?"

"The stupid peanut butter game. I'd happily open a jar of Jif if you'd like."

This is when she walks away muttering something about her life choices.

My wife complains and the kids think I'm an idiot, but we all have to make a stand at some point, and I do it on the nut butter battlefield.

Have you ever found yourself unwrapping and eating an entire Clif Bar while shopping in the supermarket and it's not until you've eaten half of it and your blood sugar settles that you realize you haven't paid for it yet and a nagging little voice in your head that sounds a lot like your mother's starts calling you a thief? I have.

But are you a criminal because you act like all this food is yours for the taking? Are you a dirty, no-good shoplifter because you never told the cashier about the Clif Bar and instead of showing her the wrapper and starting the whole transaction over again you just smiled and scanned your card? No, you're a good person, and that extra dollar you added to support St. Jude's proves it. Technically, you took something that didn't belong to you, and sure, maybe you grabbed more free cheese cube samples than you should have and scooped up some jelly beans from the bulk candy bins when no one was looking, but trust me, what you did happens all the time, so take a deep breath, smile at the security guard and hope the alarm doesn't go off when you leave the store.

When you're back in your car sitting at a red light, and you find yourself staring straight ahead but not really looking at anything and your mind drifts back to that time in high school when those bullies were picking on that kid who wore his night brace during the day and you thought that you should say something to stop them but you didn't, and all these years later you wish you could go back and protect him but then you hear car horns honking and people cursing at you, and you suddenly realize you're a grown-up driving a car and you're making everybody angry and really need to snap out of it, don't feel bad. It's totally normal. Everybody does this.

Do you feel a little better about yourself? Well, you should, because what you're doing is typical and you're no better or worse than anybody else. Have you lost track of what I'm talking about because you started thinking about dinner somewhere during the last two paragraphs and how you probably shouldn't eat so many carbs but the idea of pizza and some garlic knots sounds like something that absolutely has to be stuffed into your face as soon as possible? Yeah, that happens. Go ahead and place the order and then come back and reread what you missed.

And I know you feel bad about not having sent that thank-you note to your sister for the gift she gave you and that you really want to do it, not so much because the Santa and Mrs. Claus salt and pepper shakers were so great, but because you want her to know what a good person you are, but don't beat yourself up about it.

Everybody wants to write thank-you notes and no one does because putting an actual pen to actual paper and then finding a stamp and an envelope and licking it with your actual tongue and walking it all the way down to that ancient building they call the post office is one of the hardest things to do in life.

Sure it would be nice, but come on, she's your sister, shouldn't she already know you're thankful? And honestly, if she's mad, well, that's on her. Sisters are always blowing things out of proportion.

You'll see her at the holidays and you can give her a little extra hug so she knows you love her. Maybe you'll even get her a special gift. One that's a little nicer than the other gifts you'll give, and definitely nicer than what she gave you and costs just a little bit more and you will wrap it with a really fancy, shiny ribbon like they use on presents in the movies.

Yeah, that would be a really nice thing to do. You're always coming up with these great ideas, but for some reason always have trouble following through. You probably won't follow through on this one either, but don't worry about it, you're totally normal.

MY TOWN, YOUR TOWN, OUR TOWN

....

I live in a house, in a neighborhood, alongside other houses. I have a car in the garage and one on the street. I have a mailbox and a phone and a twisted-up garden hose covered with snails. This is where I live. This is my home. But lately I've been feeling that it's not mine at all, that I'm just the latest person who happens to get their mail delivered here, a visitor on his way to someplace else.

I didn't choose to put the doorbell there or install the porch light, and I won't be the last one to wiggle the toilet handle and reach over the sink to turn on the garbage disposal, yet on moving day it all became mine and mine alone. It's the same suspension of belief I have upon checking into a hotel when I immediately call it *my* room as if there hadn't been a thousand businessmen sleeping with the pillow between their legs before me.

Even the way the town moves, the rhythm of her intersections, the way the sun shines on certain parts of the sidewalk were all someone else's idea. But I never met any of them, so this is now *my* bank, *my* dry cleaner and *my* creepy liquor-candy-butcher-tobacco store. When I return from a trip and speed back from the airport in the rear of a cab toward more familiar ground, I tell the driver to get off at my exit that leads to my street which is really just a place where I keep all my stuff.

Most of our main streets were formed thousands of years before us by native people carving out pathways while stalking migrating herds of giant lizard creatures. Over time those paths became dirt roads covered with gravel and then cobblestones and then they were paved and repaved again and again. I don't think we need to thank the cavemen every time we take a right on red and gun it for the shopping center, but it seems respectful to once in a while keep it in mind.

There's history in every corner of every space in which we stand. As we walk down the sidewalk we are navigating through the decisions of our ancestors, who have made things both easier and more difficult for us. They expressed a thoughtfulness or a carelessness about their own lives that have now been extended to us.

Of course, they weren't thinking about us at the time. They were doing what I'm doing right now: noodling around and figuring out the best way to get through the day. They laid the flooring, ran the pipes and installed a bathroom sink that was good for them. They had no idea that sometime in the future I'd be standing naked in the very same spot brushing my teeth with something called an electric toothbrush while listening to music through something called an Alexa device.

Walk the streets of Rome and you can literally see how they lived, through the remnants of theaters, churches and walkways that were never removed. Sit by the sea in Beirut and you'll be perched on the same rocks that provided respite for people before the time of Jesus. Walk into a condo next to a strip mall in Jacksonville, Florida, and you won't feel anything at all.

Some spots seem to have a trace of every soul that was ever there. Enter into a coffee shop in Greenwich Village, a church in Antwerp or a library in London and in moments of silence and stillness you can sense that something has been left behind. There's a heartbeat in some places, and it is not our own.

Alongside the romantic spots are a lot of places that are just plain shitty where no one ever figured out the right way to do anything. These are ugly, inhospitable places and you know it the moment you cross the town line and you are greeted by a hairless stray dog walking down the middle of the street looking for a cigarette.

The signs don't make sense, you can't find a decent bench in the shade and the shops are barren, with no one around to restock the shelves. This didn't just happen. This is the result of a million bad choices by confused people who couldn't figure why they were there in the first place.

I had that experience when I was in Fresno. It's a town that was built where no one should have ever lived, and that first bad decision set off a chain reaction of misery. The valley captures the heat and smog like a broken filtration system spitting a lazy, manic haze over everyone who lives there, and it seems to drive them to madness. The old people are on drugs, the isolated form gangs and the buses are driven by pregnant teens.

As the sun went down and the temperatures cooled off by a degree or two, I decided to go for a walk outside the hotel. I got only as far as the corner before Fresno and my instinct told me not to walk on certain blocks, not just because of who might be lurking there now but because it's just one of those places where a lot of bad people do a lot of lurking.

Are there good people there? Sure. There are very nice people making very nice lives and trying their best. But it's a tough go in Fresno, the home of Sun-Maid Raisins, a dried-up fruit your face will begin to resemble if you stay there too long.

Some places are just cursed, like those buildings where the new restaurants always fail. Something is off. You can bring in the best chef in the world, create a beautiful menu in a lovely space, but some buildings don't want people in them, and the public gets the message immediately.

All this being said, I have lived in apartments that were far worse than Fresno. Places where they decided to put toilets in just the right spot so your knees hit the door. Where showerheads were installed at such a low height that even small children would have to bend over to get their hair wet.

I had one place in New York where they forgot to put a sink in the bathroom. I didn't notice it until I had moved in, because why would anyone ever look for something like that? It's not like I was looking in the paper for a one-bedroom, one-bath, sink included. That shouldn't be optional.

It wasn't until I was getting ready for bed that first night with my toothbrush in hand that I felt confused and disoriented, as if I had forgotten how this entire ritual was supposed to go. Few things will make you feel as unsettled about your life as spitting your toothpaste out around a stack of dirty dishes in the kitchen sink.

New York is legendary for horrible apartments. With space limited and rents at top dollar, landlords do all sorts of insidious things. I moved into an apartment that had such a small door it looked like the home for the Keebler Elf. It took hours of pushing, twisting and sweating before I realized that any of the furniture that was bigger than me would have to stay in the hall.

I had apartments with windows that looked out on brick walls, hallways turned into a bedroom and kitchens filled with so many rats and cockroaches running around they seemed like they'd been hired as team mascots.

I've lived in plenty of stupid places, but at some point you have to look at yourself instead of at the four walls around you. Sometimes it's the apartment, but sometimes it's you. Why am I living here? Is this just chance or is this the culmination of a lifetime of bad decisions? While I didn't technically position the window right over the garbage cans, I'm sure if we traced the steps of my life, the universe would agree that I am somewhat to blame.

People have been running around like ants trying to solve their problems for centuries. Thankfully, sometimes they get it right. Someone got the train to run through the center of the town square and someone decided to open a flower shop next to the station, alongside a hot dog stand and a pharmacy. Someone else opened a hardware store and someone a bank and together they all created a city, a place based on satisfying the needs and wants of the individual that extended to everybody else.

They painted the lines on the road and laid the paving stones. They fixed the sidewalks and kept them well-lit on the way into town. The butcher shop, the shoe repair, the watchmaker and car wash. The policeman and trash hauler and optometrist. In a good town, if you take away any one of these things, others will take it upon themselves to replace it. The profit they make is for the work they've done, but it's also a fee for having patched a hole in the torn fabric of the place we all call home.

Maybe that's our responsibility. To create some good for ourselves that will carry forward to whoever comes after us. I built a fort in the woods as a child, and when I came back from college other kids were still playing in that same spot. My friends and I built a refuge and over time other kids saw it and maintained it, made it their own and improved upon it. It's nice to think that a whole new generation has a place to hide from their parents, light off firecrackers and make up stories about the girls they made out with.

As I stand on the street outside my house, I realize that, of course, I have a responsibility to this place. To not ruin it. To be a part of it. To keep it alive. And that's why I'm going to plant a tree. I'm going to repair the mailbox and take pictures of the guy who leaves his dog's business in my yard, and post it on the telephone pole for all to see. I'm going to build a big fence so the coyotes can't come in and slaughter my pets in front of my children.

I'm going to do all of these things so the next family will thank me without ever meeting me, enjoying what I left behind and what was left to me. And I thank those before me for not building a highway through the park. Thanks for not putting the prison downtown in the lot where they sell Christmas trees. Thanks for not deciding to import alligators from Florida and put them in the fountain at the mall. While it kind of sounds fun, it wouldn't have been a good idea.

This would have been a much different place if people had installed cannons in every window and fired them off anytime someone they didn't recognize came up the street. This would have been a very different kind of town if we slaughtered animals in the town square at dusk, so thanks for putting that supermarket there instead. It's a lot more convenient and a lot less bloody.

So, yes, I live in a house, in a neighborhood, alongside other houses. I have a car in the garage and one on the street. I have a mailbox and a phone and a twisted-up garden hose covered with snails. But none of this is mine, any more than it is yours, because ultimately, neither of us will be here for long. And if you live in Fresno that's a really good thing.

DAD IS FLYING THE PLANE!

A lot of times after a show, while I'm signing books in the lobby, people will come up and tell me how crazy their family is, often while standing with that family.

"You should come over to our house if you want material. This one is certifiable," a wife will say while pointing her thumb at her husband.

"It's true," he'll chuckle.

Ask anyone about their family and they will tell you that they grew up in a house filled with crazy people. The parents were nuts, the kids were morons and everyone they visited during the holidays was out of their minds or borderline criminals.

It's funny to think that everyone's families are filled with crazy people, until you realize that these maniacs don't stay in the house. These same people who make life intolerable for everyone at home actually go out into the world, work in office buildings, run for office and drive around in police cars. They are in line in front of you at the airport, they are the voice on the phone when you call customer service and they check you in at the hotel. It's no wonder nothing works.

The pilot flying your plane is someone else's father, who, according to his daughter, is a total moron. She has lived with this man her entire life and has seen him walk into screen doors, drop his keys in the toilet and pour his coffee into a mug that's not there. She's watched as he's run around the house for twenty-five minutes looking for a phone that was right in his hand. She knows, without a doubt, that he is a bumbling idiot and that today he is going to fly a planeful of people to Cancún as fast as he can.

This is why your plane ticket is screwed up, why your pants don't fit after they've been altered and why your take-out order is missing the egg rolls. Of course the toilet doesn't work after the plumber has fixed it, because he's not just a plumber, he's also someone's dumb brother who was under your house loosening a pipe with one hand while responding to a text from his pregnant mistress with the other. How can he get this job right when he doesn't get anything right anywhere else in his life? We think we're dealing with a man who lives and breathes plumbing, but he barely even breathes.

Have you ever had your parents over on a bad day? One of those visits when they're as nutty and troublemaking as two wrinkled toddlers? Dad wanders onto the porch and stays there while Mom puts a plastic bowl full of nuts into the oven, walks into the other room and starts watering the bookshelves. It's less a visit with your parents than a very difficult babysitting shift. And then, they eventually leave, start up the car and drive out into the world, where they're no longer your problem, but everybody's problem.

That's how traffic jams build out of nowhere—goofy moms, dads and grandparents hitting the road at the same time. A mom hits the brakes, a dad swerves into the other lane, grandma forgets she's driving and before you know it we're all stuck.

The world is filled with family members on the loose. Luckily the world does a pretty good job of herding them around. The average person's day consists of getting up, going to work and back and in between looking for food. The faster we can get them back in the house, the better.

Fast food chains are a big help. The genius of McDonald's isn't its speed as much as its understanding of how dumb we all are and that it has to make the process as easy as possible. All we have to do is walk in, point at the big bright board and say a number.

Long lines are the result of asking too much of the public. Starbucks has a line out the other side of the airport because it's confusing as hell. Watching someone's mom try to place an order is like watching a pony try calculus. She locks up, sways back and forth, kicks and cries and eventually blurts something out. When she realizes she forgot to pay, she fumbles around for money, then starts pounding on the credit card machine like an ape.

The security line at the airport is epically long because the rules are changing all the time and they're asking people to undress and then put it all back together. Most people have a hard enough time getting dressed and gathering all their belongings while in the comfort of their own home with endless hours to get it done. Now they want us to undo it all, taking off belts and shoes and unpacking our bags while emptying our pockets of whatever good luck charms, loose change, metal toothpicks and doodads we've collected. Then, after this fear and humiliation we have to put it all back together, hopping around on one foot like a guilt-ridden interloper who's been caught sleeping with someone else's spouse. It's a wonder that line ever goes down at all.

No lines on earth are as long and dispiriting as the DMV's, but it's not their fault. Think of all the decisions and bits of information that are being thrown around that place. It really should be twenty different buildings, and even then it would be complicated. Everyone has a different reason for walking in there and needs different paperwork. Boats, trucks, cars, licenses, permits, smog reports, eye tests, driving tests, registration cards. Why is the lady registering to vote standing in line next to the guy who is getting his motorcycle license? This was bad planning. Every person who walks up to that window is looking for something different, and there's no way they'll have the right paperwork.

Whoever is making the credit card machines is not helping matters. Some want the card stuck in, some swiped, some tapped and some want you to use your phone. Some want it done immediately, some after the transaction and some want it left in until they can yell at you in front of everybody else in line. Some just want you to wave it in the air as if they are taking your money right from your thoughts.

All these obstacles are tough to get through, so you can imagine what happens when it's your grandmother's turn to try.

I do my best, but I know when I wander out of the house thinking I've got my act together, my kids are thinking, "Oh no, Dad's on the loose." But I don't need my family to point out all my flaws and shortcomings. I'm keenly aware of what a boob I am.

Why do I have to go back to the hardware store three times for every job? Because I know only one third of what I'm supposed to know. I know I need to fix the toilet, but I know nothing else.

And still I grab my keys with confidence and head off to the hardware store with determination and a skip in my step.

I walk in and, when they ask if they can help me, I say, "No, I'm good." As if I know more about where everything is in this store than they do. After a couple of laps I realize, "Hmmm, maybe I don't know where the toilet thingy is. Maybe I should ask, because obviously they haven't put the toilet thingy in the right place."

So I ask, "Where do you keep the toilet thingy?"

The what?

The, you know, thingy, for the toilet.

That's when I realize for the first time that I don't really know what I'm talking about at all. The manager is going to ask more questions and I'm not going to know the answers to those either.

The handle?

Yeah, with the thingy attached to the thingy.

And now I'm trying to keep up with him as he marches down the aisles and he pulls something off the shelf.

You need a fifty or a forty?

"Forty," I say with so much confidence you would think that I might have built it myself.

But of course it's not a forty, and I don't know what I'm doing or saying or even thinking at this point.

My daughters are right: I'm just a dad on the loose.

The odds are against us. How many times do you hear people say that their family is solid? That everybody knows exactly what they're doing. Dad's sharp as a tack. Mom's smart as a whip. And the kids are Rhodes Scholars. I haven't heard it once, and definitely not at Thanksgiving.

DON'T EAT THAT

....

Some rules about food.

When you're absolutely starving and you find yourself digging through the pantry like an angry raccoon, take a deep breath and remember that you're not the first person faced with this dilemma. People have been looking for lunch for centuries and have come up with some very handy rules about eating that, if followed, can eliminate a lot of your hunger pains and overall anxiety.

Some of these rules are pretty obvious. You don't eat Easter pie on Thanksgiving and you don't have meat loaf at the beach. If you're sitting poolside, grapes and sparkling water make a lot more sense than reaching into your beach bag and pouring a tall glass of lukewarm buttermilk. If this kind of behavior were at all acceptable, we'd see ads for luxury resorts featuring glamour shots of guests in hot tubs chewing on turkey legs, but we don't.

When humans got past the point of eating any animal, rodent

and bug that came down the trail whenever we could catch them, we started to develop taste and plan out our meals based on what our bodies were telling us. That's why eggs, cereal and toast make an appearance at breakfast and why you don't wake up, walk into the kitchen and start boiling a pot of lobsters. No one goes out on a date to a candlelit restaurant, secures an intimate booth in the back and orders a round of Raisin Bran. It doesn't go and it's just not right.

I've ended relationships with people just because of the way they ate. I had a friend who drank coffee with every meal. Salad and coffee, fruit and coffee, even fish with coffee. She also slapped her husband around, kept a power drill in her glove compartment and brushed her teeth with hot water. All of this makes sense, because she was a weirdo who took pride in calling herself a rule breaker, and at some point I stopped calling her.

I dated a beautiful and funny woman who dressed like a successful CEO and had the steely-eyed poise of a professional athlete. She shot pool, played darts and bet on everything, including arm wrestling. She beat men twice her size with her skinny arms, which were stronger than thick wire cables, and she was just as wily as she was strong. She'd flummox her opponents with a last-second seductive glance that reduced them to moosh, right before she pinned their arms to the table and sent them home in tears.

She was amazing. She called her breasts her "crazy aunts" and she took them out every chance she got. As my grandfather would have said, she was "a real gamer."

I loved her, but eating with her was a nightmare. She chewed so loudly that people at other tables thought she was kidding. She slurped soup, sucked on clam shells and chomped on seeds.

Patrons would look over in amazement as she shoveled food into her mouth like her face was an angry wood chipper.

But worse than her manners were her choices—she never made any. She just ate whatever she could reach, and she never stopped. If there was food around she was on it like a dog left to pour out his own portions. She'd walk into five-star restaurants eating a bag of McDonald's fries. She drank Campbell's SpaghettiOs straight from the can. She also liked to drink beers by puncturing a hole in the bottom with a key, putting the can up to her mouth, popping the top and shooting it down her throat. The kids call it "shotgunning." I call it "a weird thing to do at my sister's wedding."

Her thoughtless way of consuming food was a harbinger of things to come. The same mind that had her mix together a bowl of rigatoni with a plate of mashed potatoes and gravy also had her move out of her apartment without finding another place to live first. She never thought even one step ahead, which can be a lot of fun on spring break but is a risky game plan for the rest of your life.

The night we broke up she still spent the night because she had ordered a pizza and the delivery guy was running late.

Just follow some basic rules. Breakfast is from 6 till noon, lunch from noon to 4 P.M., dinner from 6 P.M. to 10 P.M. Any variation on these hours comes with a title needed to explain what the hell is going on: "Breakfast for Dinner," "Early Bird Special" and of course "Brunch," which is technically only on Sunday. Any breakfast or lunch combo on any other day is either a late breakfast or an early lunch. Them's the rules.

Can you have brunch on other days? Sure. You can watch a baseball game on Christmas morning, but that doesn't make it right. Brunch is the perfect smashing together of two meals on a day after a late Saturday night, when you have nowhere to be until Monday morning. That's why people don't mind standing in long lines for brunch. The whole vibe is that you have nowhere to go, which is why you grant yourself permission to order a giant Bloody Mary with bacon on a stick.

Once people started messing with brunch we ended up with the confusing excess of All-U-Can-Eat Mother's Day, Easter and jazz brunch buffets. These are good ideas gone gluttonous and rank right alongside other perversions like hot dog eating contests and six-foot party subs.

During high school I worked as a busboy at the Hilton Woodcliff Lake Hotel in New Jersey's Bergen County. They had a Sunday brunch buffet that was so popular that guests from the town who had their own houses with beds in them would rent a room for the night just so they could get a coupon for 25 percent off. I never understood the attraction. I thought the idea of eating out was that you finally got to order your own meal and no longer had to fight with the other people at the table to get fed. So why would you pay for a buffet where you now have to fend off an entire village?

The worst of human behavior is on display at a buffet. People scratch their noses and grab food with their hands rather than the tongs. People will lick syrup and other goo off their fingers, then go on to the next stop, breathing, coughing, touching and tasting everything in their path. My favorites were the people who would carry five loaded plates like hungry circus performers rather than have to make a second trip.

Just the terms they used were enough to make me never want to eat again: carving and omelet "stations," as if the guests were giant vehicles that needed to pull in and park for refueling; seafood "towers" that rose so high they scraped the ceiling; "bottomless" mimosas that sold the idea that the only end to your drinking would be puking in the fake ferns that decorated the lobby. This "mega-sized" brunch was designed to beat guests into submission with food and drink, and they loved it.

I, on the other hand, got to see up close the grotesque preparation and waste that goes into laying out food for hundreds of people all at one time. The only thing that was truly bottomless was the garbage. The end of my day was spent dragging out giant Hefty bags filled with uneaten trays of bacon, ham and floppy pancakes that left a trail of grease across the parking lot. What was presented only moments before as delicious options for the customers was now nothing more than a horrible pile of sticky congealed trash.

It took four of us to carry off the giant Poseidon-shaped ice sculpture. Even though it weighed over a hundred pounds, we were happy to move it because we knew at the end we'd get to pee on it. This wasn't required, but busboys are always looking for a good time.

I thought that the pandemic might hurt the brunch buffet business, but it didn't happen. In the same way that people flooded back onto those vile cruise ships, people are back in line with plates in hand like Oliver Twist, digging into heaps of slightly stale pastries, gummy bagels and giant bowls of flavorless fruit. Call it a swift return to our mindless normal.

One ironclad food rule that I love is that cocktail hour starts at 5 P.M. Don't let the lame T-shirts and stupid memes distract you from the fact that this is one of the strongest and wisest of all the eating and drinking rules. Starting before 5 P.M. can be done—day drinking is a thing—but this is not a wise move.

Not that I'm opposed to doing the wrong thing from time to time, but as a practice, walking out of the midday sun into a dark saloon and throwing back shots of Jack Daniel's isn't what I'd call a productive or healthy day.

Once you start drinking, pay attention to the smaller rules. When I first got into martinis I was excited. Too excited. I ordered them everywhere I went, and a lot of those places were places that you should not have been ordering a martini. I didn't know martinis came with rules, but of course they do. Don't order a martini at an Irish pub. They won't ask if you want an olive with it because they don't have olives. Don't order a martini in a decaying barroom filled with angry old men or they will punch you in the mouth. Don't order a martini at a bowling alley, a ball game or a California Pizza Kitchen.

These places, our forefathers figured out, are where you order beer. Beer is your unpretentious friend. Beer blends in. Beer doesn't impose. Beer is comfortable on a back porch, in the back of a pickup truck or in a back alley. Beer on a boat, beer at the track, beer on a hunting trip. Beer loves any place that has a dartboard, some horseshoes or a Ping-Pong table. Beer is so happy on the Ping-Pong table that we built a game around it. There's no such thing as martini pong. Martini is the show-off who needs to be the center of attention. Beer checks out Martini with his look-at-me attitude and thinks, "I bet he speaks French."

Wine isn't about being a snob; it's about drinking one of the oldest libations that humankind ever devised as a way for us to enjoy life. There is nothing snobby about drinking the stuff that Jesus drank. He was a lot of things, but he wasn't a snob, and that's saying a lot about a guy called "the Son of God."

How much wine you drink and when you drink it varies according to the culture and mood you find yourself in. My one rule is that I don't start drinking it until the cooking is complete. I've ruined many meals and melted many spatulas by clouding my precarious cooking talents with alcohol.

Deciding what and when to eat isn't all that complicated. It might have been at some point, but through trial and error and millions of upset stomachs our ancestors worked it all out.

Once, far from home at a time when leaving my young family was really difficult, I was sitting alone at a bar in Savannah, Georgia, that was known for its buffalo wings.

I'd had to fly in a day early and was looking for a reward for having survived a cross-country trip in a metal tube filled with jet fuel.

Sometimes all you have to do to get along is observe those around you. If you don't see anyone else eating a tray of lasagna by themselves with a spatula or an entire birthday cake with their hands then you might not want to either. And when you see locals in a bar enjoying wings and a local beer on tap, you just found your reward.

I put in my order with the bartender, who was cute and friendly and went out of her way to make me feel at home, which is much appreciated when you're a stranger in a strange town. I'm not looking for long-term friendships, just a pal who checks in at certain points during the meal. Sometimes all it takes is the kindness of one kid to silence the fear you have of an entire cafeteria. The bartender was that kid.

The wings were deserving of their reputation and the cold beer the perfect companion. I was following the rules of the place, eating the meal that made it famous, and the bartender gave me a beer on the house as the punctuation to a well-played meal. Everything was perfect, until I went rogue.

I pushed the gnawed-at plate of bones across the bar, chugged the last of the beer and declared a little too loudly, "Another round of wings."

As I lifted my hand to cover my burp the bartender turned from new friend to disgusted onlooker. She wasn't rolling her eyes or laughing along, she was scowling.

"Are you serious?" she asked.

"I sure am," I said even louder.

"That was enough wings for two people."

"Yepper. And another beer, thank you very much."

In an instant I went from amiable tourist to the guy who ruins a bartender's night—the moron who drinks too much and goes too far. She was mad. I had let her down. It was too late.

She gave me the silent treatment as she put the second plate down in front of me. She poured me another beer without making eye contact, because now I was an intoxicated monster who must be avoided.

She was right; of course I shouldn't have eaten a double order of wings, four beers and a shot or two. This wasn't the right way to do things. I knew that as I stumbled back to the hotel under the sad Georgia moss trees who had seen my kind many times before. I fumbled my way back into my room and collapsed on my bed, doubled over with stomach pains, drunkenness and self-pity. I pride myself on following the rules, but on that night I didn't heed a single one.

I could make all sorts of excuses as to why I lost my mind, but to be honest, I just snapped. We all do; it's human nature, and that's okay. Who knows—despite my better judgment, I may one day find myself sitting on a lounge chair at the beach under a hot tropical sun gnawing on a chunk of meat loaf. And it wouldn't be the worst thing. After washing it down with a big glass of wine all would be forgiven.

THE STUFF THAT FINDS US

....

Somewhere between those hoarders who turn their homes into recycling bins and the feng shui people who hold virtually no possessions and get angry if your chair points the wrong way are the regular people who simply collect a lot of stuff without realizing it. Some things we cherish and hold on to, some simply have got to go and others just refuse to leave.

There is a small weighted toy sitting on my desk. It's a simple metal figure on a bicycle that balances perfectly on a metal stand. It's not particularly unique or useful, but it's fun to poke him when my mind wanders and watch as, like a metallic circus performer, he wobbles back and forth and spins around without ever falling off his perch. But his most impressive trick has been his almost magical ability to remain on my desk, wherever that desk might be, since I was ten.

Money was hard to come by at that age, but whenever I got my hands on some I would spend most of it at Spencer's Gifts.

Unlike other shops at the mall, Spencer's was filled with important items like whoopee cushions, lava lamps and pens that when turned upside down revealed a lady's boobs. These things might have seemed like garbage to the adults, but to us kids, Spencer's was a gold mine.

Compared to the fake vomit and jars of slime, buying the cyclist actually seemed like a grown-up purchase. In no way did I think that he would be with me well into adulthood, but he has managed to stick around in what has now become one of my longest-lasting relationships.

He was there all through high school watching me deal with endless piles of homework. He left for a while after I graduated but then showed up again at college. I don't remember seeing him in my first apartment, but at some point he returned. I like to think that he went out on his own, maybe took a year off and pedaled through Europe, stopping for a while to take up space on someone's desk in the South of France.

Either way, he has returned once again and here he is, balancing on his metal bicycle, nodding his little round metal head as if to say, "Good to see you, old friend. *Bonjour. Avez-vous du pain?*"

My wife just cleaned out her closet for the first time in two years. It was a fraught test of logic, emotions and endurance that took three days to complete. Trying to figure out what to keep and what to toss drove her to tears. It would have been easier if she had simply had one of her kidneys removed.

We go through phases, and the clothes we collect don't change out as quickly as we do. I have a stack of cargo pants from when I thought I was going to be a hiker. I did actually hike a couple times, about fifteen years ago, and I still have the hiking boots and safari hat that went with those shorts. I keep them in my closet, because I am still that guy who thinks he's a guy who will hike the backcountry alongside wild bears and build shelters out of pine needles and make sandwiches out of moss. I am not that guy any longer—if I ever was—and even if I were, my knees aren't what they were all those years ago and all the cargo shorts in the world won't help me climb out of the parking lot onto the trail.

I still have bicycle pants with the padded shorts and European-looking jerseys left over from another identity crisis. They still sit in my drawer, because to throw them out would be admitting that I am not a cyclist, and despite having cycled for only about six months, I still feel like I kind of am.

Some clothes we live with because they are an extension of us. We picked out that shirt and bought it and it meant a lot to us. Short of the item's falling apart or falling out of fashion, the only reason to get rid of it is if it no longer fits, and even then we always believe that it will again someday soon.

Some clothing we keep just for the memories. You remember where you bought it, who kissed you while you were wearing it and how cool you used to be. I look back on certain shirts like I'm checking in on an old lover, and it takes me back to a simpler time when I truly believed, without irony, that my jean shorts were in fashion.

I have the same attachment to other items that probably should be thrown out. Books are a big one. It really takes a lot for me to remove a book from my home. Maybe it's because I also write them and the idea of someone tossing my work in the garbage or in a box on the sidewalk is devastating. Don't you dare.

Kitchen items, containers and gadgets are tough to get rid

of. You just never know when you might want to produce a Mickey Mouse–shaped waffle or give making your own ice cream another try. There have been plenty of times when I had to peel, cut or mash something and found the perfect tool at the bottom of that overflowing drawer of wacky utensils. But do I really need five different types of metal toothpicks designed specifically for martini olives? Yes. Yes, I do.

You would think that the idea that we don't live forever might speed up the de-cluttering process, but it doesn't seem to stop us. The ancient Egyptians were buried with all their favorite things, jewelry and pets included. We scoff at such an idea, but if the people who built the pyramids thought that their jewelry might have a soul and travel with them to the great beyond, who are we to dispute it?

The "last will and testament" is a list of all the stuff that you just know everyone is going to want despite the fact that they probably won't. I know it's hard to believe your heirs won't be interested in going through your old calendars to see that dentist appointment you had in 2011, but it's true.

Attics and garages are filled with stuff we'll never use. Footballs, Frisbees, paddleball paddles. I would throw all of it away, but my wife has other ideas. It's no surprise that the same woman who stood in her closet in a catatonic state while holding a blouse from the early 2000s refuses to let me toss a broken pogo stick because it reminds her of when our daughter couldn't figure out how to pogo-stick.

The attachment to anything that the children touched, used or thought about is incredibly powerful and debilitating when one is trying to clean up the house. There sits on my dresser a misshapen ball of clay that one of our daughters made about a hundred years ago. To this day no one knows what it is or even what it was supposed to be. It looks like it may have started out as an animal, turned into a building in the shape of a person and then was stepped on with the heel of a boot and ended up as some sort of sick and misshapen creature. It was painted yellow with a little blue mixed in, which made most of it a dark brownish swirl.

Everyone who sees this child-art has their own interpretation, as if they are describing a cloud, but one thing is certain—there's no need to keep it. The artist, my oldest, has no memory of making it. My wife tries to lay claim to some distant memory of when it came into the house, but her story has changed enough for me to know that she is making it up. All she knows is that one of our children made it a long time ago, and therefore it lives on as a representation of that fun, chaotic time of our young family life and to discard it would be admitting and declaring out loud that that period is over and will not be coming back.

These items are the totems or mile markers of our lives. But in practical terms there comes a time when we have to let some of it go. Sometimes you have to move on. If the children are now using their beloved plastic toy kitchen to clean their marijuana and roll joints, perhaps it's time to bring it to Goodwill.

But I don't feel that all things are meaningless. Some of our belongings carry a spirit, a memory that's so strong that it seems to embody the object. I have a porcelain mug that I gave to my grandmother when I was eleven. It's burnt orange and has an etching of a small German cottage nestled on the side of a brook. The mug itself isn't anything special, but I stole it from a gift shop during my short shoplifting phase. It wasn't a phase that lasted very long, but it was very exciting, and before it ended—when my friend Keith and I were kicked out of a record store by the owner, who suspected that we were about to steal the new Police album—I successfully lifted this German cup and then gave it to my grandmother.

She never knew that I'd stolen it, but she knew I was proud of the gift, and that in turn made her give it a special place on her shelf of keepsakes. Every time I would sit in her living room during one of our visits, I would see the little mug and smile to myself, proud that somehow, without any money or job or mode of transportation greater than a bicycle, I was able to get such a nice present for my nana and make her happy. This is probably similar to what the guys in the Mafia think about when they look around their living rooms.

That mug has a story with multiple meanings, interpreted by both of us, and is more important than other things I'm sure I gave her or she gave me. It is a keepsake, and it now sits on a shelf in my office, and if the owner of the record shop ever solves the crime and shows up at my house, he'll never take me alive.

I had a jean jacket once. It was the coolest jacket I ever owned. My girlfriend put patches on it and it had excellent secret inside pockets and looked and smelled like I had really traveled. Like I had really lived. It told people that I had been around the world, slept in fields in the South of France and ran from trouble in Germany and down broken Turkish streets. In reality it never got out of New Jersey—but it looked and smelled like it did.

It wasn't just a jacket. It was a part of me. An important part of me that I think I left on a fishing boat or maybe it was stolen at a party or left in my friend's car by mistake. As much as I loved it, it was one of those items that knew when it was time to go.

Most things are pretty meaningless, and we buy them with the full understanding that they won't be around for long. Sunglasses rarely make it through an entire summer without evaporating into the ether. It's not their fault; they're more a victim of one of life's unsolvable problems.

People invite you to a barbecue. It starts around four. The sun is out and it will be bright for quite some time. You're going to need your sunglasses for the next three hours as you enjoy yourself with some fun rum drinks, a couple hot dogs and maybe a jump in the pool.

After all of this activity you are no longer in the same state of mind that you were when you walked in, with your sunglasses sitting safely on your nose. Now, drunk, gassy and soggy, with the sun going down, you will have to do the impossible—remember your sunglasses.

You have a better chance of hanging on to them if you paid too much for them, which is any amount that makes you feel a little embarrassed if someone asks what they cost. If you paid too little for them, which is any amount less than your average slice of pizza, it lowers how much you care and the amount of time before you lose them. I have a drawer filled with sunglasses that were abandoned at my house and not once have I gotten a call or a question from someone trying to retrieve them, because they're cheap and silly and disposable just like lighters, pens and lip balm.

And yet some items, regardless of what they cost, have a way of following you around for years. They magnetically return to you again and again, like a lost puppy or a long-lost friend who just through their resilience and loyalty win their way into your heart. Like my trusty metal cyclist.

Intermittently I'll tap it as I always have and get it rocking back and forth. I can twirl it, rock it or knock it around and it seldom falls off its perch. It's one of those desktop toys that occupies a busy mind in between more important tasks like writing, paying bills or daydreaming about life. I wonder how those daydreams have changed from the mind of that ten-year-old kid to this middle-aged father of two.

I don't clearly remember what that ten-year-old was thinking when he mindlessly spun the cyclist around in between homework assignments, but I know he wasn't thinking about me. He had no idea that this man with thinning hair was going to be living clear across the country, with a family and pets and a mortgage. He had no way of knowing the losses we'd suffer or the joys that we'd have or the bread that we'd bake.

I know he was at once worried and fearless. I also remember that he had a real faith in things and desperately wanted to understand and capture the world by holding it as tight as he could. He believed that life was something permanent and knowable and that he desperately wanted to gain control over it, in the same way his father seemed to be doing.

As I tap the cyclist now with my pen, I'm wondering how much easier it would have been if I'd been able to tell the younger me that none of that control he yearned for was even possible. That trying to get a grip on this ever-changing world is like trying to grab hold of an ocean wave. Maybe it would have helped to ease his fears and calm him down. Or maybe some things are better figured out by oneself.

And besides, why bother him at his desk? I'm sure he had enough on his mind already, as he spun his little metal friend around, wondering how to graduate, how to get a girl and how to find a really cool jacket.

QUIT COMPLAINING

....

"Stop whining. No one likes it when you complain."

I'm not sure who to attribute this bit of wisdom to, but it's been repeated by some of the greats: both my grandmothers, my friend's dad and Carol, the fun cashier at the supermarket with all the pins on her apron and a name tag that read, "Carol," with a bright yellow sun for the *o*.

It's a truism that should be told to all the people in all the lands. It should be printed on T-shirts, made into bumper stickers and scrawled across the bottom of CNN under "Breaking News." It needs to be heard, understood and followed, because if it's not, and you wander around complaining all the time, you will eventually find yourself alone, in a sad little apartment, whining to the only friend left in your life, a water bug who lives in a crack in the floor just under the sink.

Complaining is saying out loud what we're all going through but have the decency and better judgment to keep to ourselves.

Everyone has a long list of complaints, so what gives you the right to dump yours onto us? No one wants you adding to our troubles with your bellyaching about how bad traffic was or how your eyeball has been twitching for weeks. We don't need to hear about your leaky roof or what your stomach feels like after too many waffles. We've got our own stomachs to deal with.

I don't complain because I grew up with a lot of other people and learned from a very early age that I wasn't special. It became very clear that I was just another one of what everybody else was, so why would my troubles be unique?

Things haven't been going your way recently? Join the crowd.

You've had a bad day at work? Who didn't?

You feel like no one likes you, including you, and that you are totally alone? That's life, kid; now clam up and pass the potatoes.

I'm one of twenty-one grandchildren. I once got a birthday card from my grandmother that was addressed to "Tammy." She didn't know my name. She didn't even know I was a boy. To me she was my special grandmother, but to her I was just another vague blur of hair and acne looking for something to eat.

And why should she be expected to know every detail about each of her grandchildren? She was about 150 years old, had one hip, three hairs on her head and a thin candy coating for skin. There wasn't anything we could complain about that would gain her sympathy.

She used to say, "I lived through two World Wars and the Great Depression, and this is what I get: I look like hell and my eyes leak."

And they did. Not at night, not sometimes, but basically all the time, right there in front of everybody. I would never compare my grandmother to an aging pug, but if anyone did they wouldn't be wrong. Life is hard.

One good thing about getting lost in a big family is that it makes you work incredibly hard. If you want to feel good about yourself you have to go out and really achieve something. Entire cities were built by men and women whose parents didn't notice them. When you don't receive blind approval from your parents or your teachers, you just keep pushing and racing and building, and before long you've made a rocket ship that's shot into space with your name on it.

But the reality is that we all lose in life most of the time. It's okay. Those are the odds. Winning is something special that happens only once in a while and mostly to other people. That's why we get so excited when someone is victorious. All around the world stadiums are filled with millions of people who sacrifice their own time and money in the hopes of watching someone actually pull through in the end and win at something. We'll watch whatever you've got: cricket, football, Ping-Pong, cornhole, video games. Just show us there's a chance that it all might work out.

Equally as satisfying and intriguing is watching the losers. How are they going to handle the defeat, the humiliation, the hurt that we all know too well? Will they lose with dignity or freak out and throw their clipboard across the room into the back of a reporter because they just can't take it anymore?

I had a couple bad moments playing Little League. Once, after getting thrown out at home plate, a devastating event for a ten-year-old, I stood up and threw my batting helmet into the fence and swore like I was in a Tarantino movie. The crowd grew more and more quiet with every vile word I yelled, until I realized I had made an official spectacle of myself. As I stood there panting and foaming at the mouth, parents shook their heads, the ump yelled at me and my father grabbed me by the arm and made me apologize to the bleachers. There's nothing like public humiliation to let you know there is a more graceful way to accept defeat.

Don't complain. The last thing we need is a play-by-play of how much harder your life is than anyone else's. For a while my wife started off every morning like a foul-mouthed rooster, sitting up and swearing at the sky. She wasn't even aware that she was doing it, until I pointed out that this might not be the healthiest start to the day. Mornings are tough for everyone. The only people who don't have trouble waking up in the morning are the ones who are still in bed.

Kids complain a lot, which is natural, because they need adults to fix everything for them and complaining is how they communicate. When you're too young to cook and have no money to go to McDonald's on your own, you should be allowed to tell your mother that her fish sticks suck. But at a certain point it has to stop, because beyond Mom and Dad the list of people who truly care about you is really short.

The only thing worse than complaining is bragging. There's nothing wrong with thinking highly of yourself and believing that you'll do great things, if that's what gets you out of bed in the morning, but a little humility when you are speaking to other people will help you avoid being punched in the face.

We ran into a couple we know, and right after the greetings they told us they'd just bought an island. Who opens a conversation like that? That's like opening your bankbook and saying, "Look how much money we have! We know you have to worry about health care and putting your kids through college and where you're going to end up when you're old, but we don't!"

Bragging actually does the same thing to people that complaining does—it makes them run away from you.

Complaining isn't only bad for other people—it's bad for you. You start to convince yourself that things are supposed to go wrong. It becomes a part of your act, and the universe starts to play along.

One of the nicest things you can say about someone is that they never complained. It's like announcing a major accomplishment. After someone dies you'll hear about how they were sick for years, and had every reason to complain but didn't. I had an aunt like that.

"Aunt Teresa died."

"What? How?"

"She had cancer for years. You knew that."

But I didn't know that. Nobody knew that. She never told me. All she said was how badly she wanted to make out with my friends, right up to the very week she died. That's a trouper who should be honored for her bravery, her nobility and, at the very least, her ability to not be annoying.

I have a friend whose father used to tell people about how sick he was only after he was better.

"Man, I was sick as a dog yesterday. I couldn't breathe, my head was pounding and I couldn't remember my name. So, what's for dinner?"

I've adopted this technique, and it really works. People are grateful when they hear that I went through something disgusting, took care of it myself and now I'm ready for some fun. No one minds hearing about your hardships when they're over, because now they don't have to help you.

If you tell a story about a rat that crawled up your leg on the subway and it ends with the rat biting you on the testicle and now you're convinced you have rabies and need a ride to the hospital, we're recoiling. But if you tell the same exact story and you've already been to the doctor and he put your testicle in a sling, we're laughing with you, because we weren't involved in the ending. We didn't have to drive you anywhere, fill out any forms or construct a tiny ice pack. All we had to do was listen to a funny story. But keep in mind that our laughing will stop immediately if you start complaining that your testicle sling is too tight.

CATS—ANCIENT MENACE

....

They say that, if left alone, your cat will eat you after you die. I know mine would, and not because he's heartless, but because cats do what's most practical, and if I don't appear up to the task of feeding him, he'll simply make other plans. If this comes as a surprise to you, you may have been conned by the cats in your life into thinking they are passive, loving creatures as opposed to the con artists they are.

Allow me to fill you in on some other cat behavior that, while not as gruesome as turning you into an entree, is still quite disturbing, and makes one wonder why humans have maintained a relationship with cats for thousands of years.

Your cat is changing your passwords.

Have you ever logged into one of those accounts that you don't use all the time but use often enough that you should remember the password and you realize you don't and you check the spot where you keep your passwords and lo and behold you did remember it and it *still* doesn't work? Who could have changed it? How did this happen? It was your cat.

Not only that—cats use your computer to spread rumors about you online. They open fake Facebook accounts and fold the gossip in among political-conspiracy rants and questionable Web searches. Before logging off they also order things on Amazon. When you get a delivery and can't remember when you ordered an entire bag of pom-poms, don't be alarmed. You're not losing it. You just have a cat.

A cat will mess with your scale.

You do your best—you diet, you exercise, you cut down on alcohol—and still you gain weight. How can this be? Why are you such a big, fat loser? Well, it's not you, it's your scale, and your scale is being altered by your cat. Cats deploy their unique cat-arm-flexibility, normally used for taunting you under the bathroom door while you sit on the toilet, to reach under the scale and twist the dial just enough so you feel like a failure, give up and eat another bowl of ice cream. Then, when you are disgusted and toss the spoon in the sink, guess who licks it clean?

They cancel your shows.

Cats love true crime. They simply can't get enough of any form of entertainment that features all the horrible things that can happen to people. They listen to podcasts, read about them online and love watching shows about it. They're obsessed. Not only is it entertaining, but it enables them to learn all the ways that you can die, which would interfere with their feeding until—as I said earlier—they use you as cat food.

So don't be surprised when the DVR stops recording right before the big reveal on your favorite house renovation show. Someone, aka your cat, interrupted your recording in favor of what they wanted to watch, and as any true crime fan knows, this was not an accident.

They will ruin your brand.

You're going for modern cool and your pants are now covered in fur. You are trying for youthful and energetic and you have bags under your eyes and scratch marks on your face from the sneak attacks in the middle of the night. Cats don't want you to have a new brand. Your brand was created the minute you brought the cat home—Cat Lady. Deal with it.

They won't invite you to anything. Ever.

Cats do stuff. They go places, watch movies and work on puzzles. They have parties under the comforter, sleepovers in the den and tanning sessions on the floor. Have they ever once asked you to come along? No. And don't confuse their demand for play as an invitation. It's not.

Cats love to move your phone.

Not far, just far enough that you think you have early signs of dementia. How many times have you found your phone on the edge of the tub, dangerously close to a water glass, or in the refrigerator and said out loud, "Who put this here?" Do you notice that your cat doesn't answer? Of course she doesn't; she's not a liar, she's just manipulative.

They kick you out of the house.

Do you ever wonder why you crave a trip to a place you've never been before? Do you think these thoughts of wanderlust just drop into your head out of nowhere? No, they do not. They are cultivated from kitten whispers. As soon as you nod off with a cat on your lap, he starts in with the soft-spoken suggestions: "The Maldives. Go to the Maldives. You deserve to be able to tell people you've been to the Maldives." Before you know it, you're grabbing your passport, filling up his bowl and leaving the cat in the house by himself.

Well fed. For now.

DON'T SWIM ALONE

Sometimes my childhood could be so boring that I would get excited to pack my little suitcase and spend the night at a seventy-year-old woman's house. It doesn't sound so great right now, but as a ten-year-old kid who rarely traveled as far away as the Dairy Queen, sleeping at my grandmother's house was a really fun getaway.

I felt important there in a way I didn't at home. In my house it was clear that I was a small part of a much bigger place, but at Nana's I was an honored guest.

"Oh, look who's here—my Tommy!" she'd say as she hugged me and took my bags like an eager bellhop at a fancy hotel.

"Right this way. I'm so excited. We've got so many plans." She was also a great concierge.

She had the energy of a hummingbird. Her house was small, almost kid-sized. It had little rooms, smaller appliances and a tiny refrigerator with just enough milk and butter to get through the day. Even the door handles were lower, giving me the powerful feeling that I had grown just by walking in. It was as if the house had been designed to make growing children and shrinking old people equally comfortable.

As she tucked me into the tiny bed that pulled out of the tiny couch in the tiny den, she told me that tomorrow was a big day because we were going to Aunt Anita's house to play bridge with her "lady friends."

She was always playing cards. She played bridge with other adults, Go Fish and Kings in the Corner with us kids and Solitaire when no one could take it anymore. She was a card shark dressed as an Italian grandmother.

Her Lady Friends, as she called them, were a fun crew of gals who grew up in Jersey City during Frank Sinatra's heyday. They lived through the Great Depression, World War II and a bunch of assassinations, so nothing really surprised or bothered them anymore. Her response to any problem thrown her way was "That's life."

They also grew up in a time without television, so she loved games like charades and bridge and drinking. The bridge game was a weekly affair that was set in stone. For this generation, plans were not fluid commitments that changed depending on mood, energy or better offers. If you said you were coming over for dinner, you came over for dinner. If you had a bridge game on a late Wednesday morning, you showed up despite having to drag a confused, uncomfortable child with you.

I wasn't happy about the plan to go to Aunt Anita's. I wanted my grandmother all to myself. I looked forward to sitting at the kitchen table and eating her signature lunch: a baloney sandwich on white bread with a pickle on the side. It wasn't so much the sandwich that I enjoyed as much as being alone with her at the table, without my sisters or parents getting in the way. I could sit at the head of the table, munching on a kosher dill, as if I were the most important person in the world.

She could sense any disappointment I ever felt and would try to smooth things over. Adults were always trying to upsell a bad situation in order to appease a child. "We're going to your aunt's house, but they have a dog." Or "We're driving three hours out to Long Island to see an uncle you haven't met, but he has a swing set."

The upsell on the trip to Aunt Anita's was that she had a pool. This was big. We didn't know any private-pool people. We were public-pool people. People we knew got in the car and went to pools in public places filled with sweaty strangers. We were public-pool people who fled our fan-cooled homes, bought badges, pinned them to our bathing suits and found chairs among the other hot, sweaty people from the town. But not tomorrow!

The plan was that I would get to swim while the Ladies played cards. Tossing me in the pool was a convenient way to get rid of me while they gambled, ate little sandwiches and got drunk on wine before noon. It sounded like it might be okay, but as with all things presented by old people, I was suspicious. I wondered what the catch would be.

With adults there was always a catch. The aunt's dog would bite children, or the swing set was really a ball. I was prepared that maybe it wasn't really a pool at all. Maybe it was a tub that they would try to convince me was a pool. That sounded about right. I'd be forced to get into my bathing suit and have to sit in a tub while a group of old ladies gathered around.

We got to Aunt Anita's house at around ten, lunchtime for the old gals. Everything is done a little earlier when you're old.

Lunch at ten, dinner at five. When you have very little to do between meals, there's not much point in waiting around.

After a quick hello and the usual round of "He's so big" and "He's so handsome" and some innuendo I was too young to understand but kind of understood, they led me out to the pool. As cute as I must have been, they wanted me out of their hair so they could play their game and talk about their husbands and money and whatever it is that old Lady Friends chat about. They didn't need ten-year-old Tommy hanging around.

One of my favorite things about New Jersey in the height of the summer is that it's bursting with green. Giant maple and oak trees with fresh new leaves combine with luxuriant grass to create a heaving green tribute to summer's fullness. Don't let the New Jersey Turnpike fool you—this state can be heart-breakingly beautiful.

Aunt Anita's yard was so filled with trees that the pool was nowhere in sight. I was led along a slate walkway through tall, unmowed grass, the morning dew soaking my sneakers and the bottoms of my tube socks. We went around the bend, up some steps . . . and there was the pool.

It was real. Not only was it a private pool, but it was a large, in-ground pool. The private pools in our town were aboveground and looked cheap and makeshift. I once watched my neighbor's aboveground pool break open and spit my babysitter out onto the lawn like a sponge from a bucket. An in-ground pool is like the Rolls-Royce of pools. Aunt Anita must have been rich.

There was even a separate pool house, a cabana really, where a young man could enjoy some privacy while he was changing. "It's not heated, but it will be fine." I put my hand into the water. It was cold. Really cold. This was the catch, but I didn't care.

They showed me where everything was and left me to change into my bathing suit and enjoy myself in the unheated water. On a hot summer day, late in the afternoon, this would have been perfect. On this cool morning it was clammy and cold and I suddenly felt alone in the woods. Complaining would do me no good. You don't complain about an in-ground pool to a group of Rosie the Riveter, Depression-era dames.

I went into the cabana, into a smallish changing area that closed with a curtain so that you could see people only from their knees down. This was no doubt designed as a way to prevent people from having sex there. For a ten-year-old boy it was almost waist-high, so I was happy to be alone as I changed into my bathing suit.

A quick word on bathing suits of the time. This was the seventies, when they still hadn't perfected many things. Cars were big and moronic, televisions looked like suitcases and suitcases didn't have wheels. With so little mastery of the big things, no one was spending much time on improving the bathing suit. They were made out of a coarse, thick material that was highly absorbent and soaked up water like a sponge. One dip in the pool and your shorts started to drown you. The only thing holding them up was a rope belt of the sort that was more commonly used for a bag of onions or a sack of volleyballs.

I quickly put my suit on and was getting excited that despite being a little chilly I was about to swim in a pool all by myself. I couldn't believe they were letting me do it. They didn't know if I could swim, how good a swimmer I was or if I would be able to save myself from my twenty-five-pound weighted swim trunks, and they didn't care. They came from a "Fend for yourself" generation. I came from a "Please help me" generation.

I was a nervous kid, or what was described back then as a

"nervous wreck." This was a time when there was no diagnosis, no therapy, no attempt at even explaining most human conditions. People just laughed at you and called you names, and I was called a nervous wreck. They were right.

I worried about everything: I worried about going places. I worried about coming back. I panicked over things that really shouldn't have worried a young child. Things like the mail and phone calls and parking spaces. I worried we wouldn't find a space and then when we did I was worried that it was illegal and we were going to be towed. I was always reading and rereading the parking signs, convinced that when we returned to our car it would no longer be there and we would spend the rest of the night trying to get it back from the Mafia, who would hold it hostage behind a chain-link fence and say things like "It's out of my hands" and "You'll have to wait till tomorrow for when the boss comes back." A six-year-old shouldn't be thinking about stuff like this.

This nervous state was a manifestation of my parents' anxieties, of which I was highly aware. When in doubt, blame the parents. My father's contribution to my anxiety was his intense rage against anything that came at us from the outside world. Parking meters, tolls, traffic, highways, cities, trains and airports were not just unreasonable obstacles designed to ruin his good time but tools sent by the universe to destroy us. He made it seem like leaving the house was the stupidest thing we could do and that everything would be ruined by "all those dickheads" out there.

Parades were filled with "too many jackasses trying to get close." A trip to the city was "bumper-to-bumper traffic filled with people who don't know how to drive." Going to church was "a living hell and there was no way we would ever get a goddamned seat."

Every flight would be canceled, every train would be late and every parking lot would be full, except for the one run by those crooks, who charge a hundred bucks and lock up the lot before we want to leave.

This was not quiet anxiety that he would keep to himself. My dad would erupt and yell and scream about it at every opportunity: before he left, when he was there and when he came back, at which time my mother would wail along in disbelief.

She'd pick up the phone: "They canceled your flight? Oh, my God! How are you going to get home? Your father is stuck at the airport in Chicago! A snowstorm? Oh my God, he's stuck in a blizzard and the storm's headed this way! We may never see your father or his luggage again!"

And this is why at six years old I started shaking like a leaf whenever my father parallel-parked in New York City.

I wet the bed, and when I wasn't wetting the bed I was sleepwalking. And not sleepwalking like taking a pleasant stroll around the house mumbling funny incoherent phrases. I would apparently walk out of my bedroom inconsolably screaming and moaning. My mother thought I was possessed. My father thought I was intentionally ruining his sleep.

When I didn't get up sobbing in the middle of the night, I stayed under the covers and peed all over myself, unaffected or bothered until the next morning. It's a terrible feeling when you wake up and are instantly humiliated by behavior that you knew nothing about and had no control over. A lot like being Catholic.

I don't remember the peeing, but I do remember the embarrassment. The puzzled looks on my parents' faces as to why their son was wetting the bed like an infant in the night. The times I had to sit on the table in the doctor's office as my mother and the doctor discussed what was wrong with me as if I weren't there. I remember the doctor suggesting I stop drinking water altogether and that my mother buy some rubber sheets.

It's funny that my current doctor asks how many times I get up to pee at night as he looks for clues about my aging prostate. When I say I get up three times to pee he's unhappy with the answer, but I'm proud that at least I made it to the bathroom.

So as I came out of the cabana, preparing to swim alone, it took real courage to follow through. I was thinking about all sorts of things that could go wrong. What if my hand got stuck in the filter and wouldn't let me go? What if I was so fat that I wouldn't float? What if a water snake somehow got in the pool and bit me in the penis?

These fears were not unfounded. Everyone I knew had heard the story of the kid who got bit on his penis by a snake. It was one of those stories that kids talked about in hushed tones while drinking a Coke on the way to the public pool.

More often than not I was afraid of all the things that could go wrong because, like a family curse, many times they did go wrong. Like a wolf in the wild or a soldier at war, I sensed danger and trusted my instincts.

So as I stood at the edge of the pool staring at the silent black water, I began to talk myself out of danger. There was no one there to cheer me on or make me feel stupid for not jumping in. It was up to me alone to gain my own strength and courage, despite my neuroses warning me not to do it.

Sometimes our overall sense of danger doesn't help us to pinpoint where the fear is coming from. We can't imagine what is about to happen, so we simply cast the fear off as irrational nonsense. And what could be more irrational than not jumping in a pool that I had all to myself?

I took a few steps back and in a mad, inspired rush ran as fast as I could, jumped off the edge of the pool and hit the freezing-cold water. My body instantly convulsed in shock. Why did I do this?! My giant sponge bathing suit was pulling me down. I was in trouble. I was drowning. There was no one around to save me. I knew this would happen. I kicked and flapped in every direction. It was so cold. Somehow I got to the surface. There was air. I might live. I took in a deep, lifesaving breath and I instantly shit my pants.

Literally.

This was bad. This was really bad. I raced to the ladder. In my mind I was back in the public pool filled with mean kids and parents and supercool lifeguards and every girl I ever knew or saw or hoped to impress.

I was horrified. I scurried up the ladder as I felt something big in my shorts that wasn't there before and was making my bathing suit even heavier. I waddled around in circles, duck-legged and confused, not knowing what to do. I somehow made my way to the cabana, just as my suit hit the floor.

I stood naked in disbelief, horrified at myself. How could I have done this? I knew something was going to go wrong, but not this! I never would have guessed *this.* How could anyone have guessed this? Suddenly, drowning didn't seem so bad.

What was my next move? Walk back into the house and hold up my soiled suit for the Lady Friends? "Hey gals, look what I just did. The rule was only 'No *peeing* in the pool,' right?"

There was no running water in this cabana. I had no options. I balled up the suit and threw it into the woods, or, more accurately, the leaves on the side of the pool. I can only imagine how far my little arms threw it—probably no more than a foot or two. Someone was sure to find it, but that wasn't my problem. My problem was getting the hell out of there as quickly as possible without having to produce the bathing suit, but a lost article of clothing was not something that Depression Nana would let slide.

It was time to lie. Lie and keep lying and don't stop lying until we were back in the car riding away to safety. I walked into their card game and started with the reliable childhood fib that my stomach hurt. I lied that I thought I was getting sick. I begged to go home.

I even lied that I hadn't gone swimming.

"Why is your hair wet?"

"Is it?"

"Yes, it is."

"Can we go?"

"Where's your bathing suit?"

"Can we go?"

"Okay, fine, we'll go, but where's your bathing suit?"

I didn't have anything to say. My pea brain couldn't come up with another story, so I just froze. I froze and stared, cheeks turning red, and waited for whatever came next.

She looked at me for a long agonizing moment. I was caught. I saw it in her eyes. She knew I was lying.

"Okay, let's go."

My grandmother didn't know that I crapped myself like an infant in a rush of nervousness and that I defiled her friend's pool. She didn't know that in my panic the only good idea I could come up with was to fling my dirty suit into the ivy and that it was there waiting for her Lady Friends. All she knew was that I had done something, I was in trouble and it was her job to save me, without judgment. That's the joy of being a grandparent—you get all the heroism of airlifting everyone out of disaster while leaving the dirty work of discipline to the parents.

My grandmother didn't ask any prying questions on the ride home. Rather, she filled the awkward silence with talk about her friends and what we were going to have for lunch, and that if we had time maybe we'd go see a movie. *The Bad News Bears* was playing at the Majestic, the same theater where we saw *Herbie the Love Bug*.

"That could be fun!" She smiled.

I couldn't talk.

Every once in a while she'd look over to see if she had successfully restored my spirit. I just nodded along, trying my best to fight back tears brought on by a flood of emotions that I couldn't understand. I was being showered with all this kindness and understanding after I'd done something so humiliating, so horrible. None of it made any sense.

Back at the house, eating my baloney sandwich, I started to feel better. She didn't ask me what had happened, she didn't ask if I wanted to talk. She just gave me an extra pickle, shuffled the cards, split the deck and dealt me in.

THE LESSON OF MARK TWAIN'S CIGARS

While traveling through upstate New York on an early winter morning, I took a detour to visit Mark Twain's writing study, which sits on the campus of Elmira College after being moved from its original location on a farm where Twain—born Samuel Clemens—summered at his in-laws' house. His sister-in-law had it built for him, which could be seen as a loving gesture, but it's more likely that she desperately wanted to get rid of him.

The writing study is an octagonal, eight-by-eight, free-standing structure, like an enclosed gazebo. It has windows all around, a fireplace and of course a writing desk. But it's what sits on that desk that really caught my eye: Twain's ashtray. According to the nearby museum, he smoked up to *thirty* cigars a day. It was the moment I learned this that I recognized his real genius—the art of being alone.

It is my belief that Mark Twain, this incredibly sensitive and observant mind, didn't really smoke all those cigars. If he had, he would have been dead before the third chapter of *Huckleberry Finn*. No, he didn't smoke them, but he lit every single one of them. He lit them up like bug-repellent citronella candles and created such a despicable fog that he forced his family to build him a hut, kick him out of the house and give him the solitude he needed to work.

Brilliant.

If he had stayed in that house, he wouldn't have gotten anything done. All those novels, all those lectures and all those witty lines that he endlessly gave to the world would have been lost. Everyone has to get out of the house, because if you don't, the house will swallow you whole, like a black hole filled with leaky sinks, needy pets and crying babies.

If there's any doubt that your home is complete chaos, just take inventory of all the items in it and try to remember how even a fraction of them got there. Every article has a story attached, and yet I don't remember buying half of them. Where did these spoons, books and salt packets come from? All this cleaning stuff and mountains of power cords? I'm sure if we went through the bills, it would prove I bought them and carried them into the house, but I'm telling you, Your Honor, I have no memory of any of it.

A lot of things accumulate as a reaction to the endless emergencies that are hammering us all the time. Go through a family's medicine cabinet and closets, and you will find piles of stuff that were brought into the home to solve a problem or save someone's life.

Every old package of Benadryl is the reaction to a mystery allergy attack that sent the family into a red alert. Our most recent averted tragedy was when my wife came down with a surprise rash in the middle of the night. We had no idea what caused it—the wine, a spider?—and we had no time to figure it out. Her body was rebelling and trying to get our attention by creating a thousand red bumps on her torso. We did the only thing we could do: run to the all-night pharmacy and get a box of that miracle drug, Benadryl.

I don't know how this stuff works, but it does. And not only in calming down a raging rash but in making me feel like a hero—as if I did something more than dash out to CVS in the middle of the night with no shoes on. Every time I cure someone with Benadryl, I feel like part doctor, part Liam Neeson.

Living with a family is like running an inner-city emergency room. As soon as you patch someone up from a skateboard accident, the next bleeding victim comes in straight from the trampoline. And whatever you used to nurse someone back to health you hold on to, because if it happened once it will happen again.

We have boxes on the shelves filled with expired medicine that will be there for the rest of our lives. There's a half bottle of NyQuil from that cough the kids caught, piles of antacids, sinus sprays, twenty boxes of Sudafed and for some reason, a giant bag of unopened cotton balls from the early nineties.

And the medicine cabinet contains just a fraction of the evidence that home is an insane place filled with nonstop action. There's stuff left over from parties and car repairs and holiday decorating. If we threw out every box of holiday decorations, we would have enough room for three more kids. Walking into our storage closet off the garage is like walking through Party City. Giant plastic skeletons lean against dust-covered Easter baskets and dirty wire reindeer. As soon as one holiday is over, we're unpacking the next and trying to stuff the old one back into the boxes it came from, which, for some reason, never fits.

Closets are filled with office stuff, envelopes and fifty different types of paper. I have no idea where all the paper clips came from. I swear that I have never bought a paper clip or a rubber band in my life and still they're all over the house! I'm like a human magnet that attracts anything remotely resembling a twist tie.

The garage is filled with abandoned instruments, sporting goods, microphones and art books. Paints, dance stuff and a heavy bag. There's discarded horse riding stuff, baseball gloves and gymnastics equipment. You'd think we were running a YMCA when actually we just ran out to the sporting goods store anytime someone mentioned they might have an interest in something, in hopes that they were developing a passion for anything other than drugs.

There are dog carriers, extra litter boxes and dog toys. Cat toys, old carpet-covered scratching posts and abandoned aquariums that we're keeping for when we get another fish someday, which we'll never do because no one here likes fish. I recently found three unlabeled boxes in my office closet that turned out to be the ashes of three dead pets. Rather than burying them in the yard, we turned them into more clutter.

That's a house. A giant place filled with clutter, worry, joy and concern. I wouldn't change it for anything, but I also wouldn't try to write the next great American novel there either. Only a fool would attempt to write anything longer than an email at home and only a genius like Mark Twain would figure a way to get kicked out of his own house.

He wasn't sweeping the porch and cleaning the gutters. I bet you never saw his legs sticking out from under the sink while he went to work on a clogged drain. No, this great mind knew that a house is an ongoing project best avoided.

There are garage doors that won't open right, leaks that can't be found and never-ending sounds of trouble. There are invasions by bugs and raccoons and your neighbor's children. Someone is going to smash a glass while someone else spills some syrup and someone else stuffs something into the toilet. The problems from one single toilet can eat up years of your life.

"Why is it making that noise? Why is it still running? Who tried to flush a dish towel?"

That's why we all need to run away from home now and again. We need to give ourselves mental freedom from everyone and everything that depends on us. Maybe not to write novels for the masses, but to make sense of our own stories. Pen may never hit paper, but your mind will go to work, tell tales about where you have been and give you clarity and hope about where you are headed.

All our major life events—falling in love, losing a job, the death of someone close to us—eventually get settled into the story of our lives. We edit them and shuffle the facts around, but eventually these are the stories we carry with us and tell people even when they didn't ask.

So get out of the house, light up a cigar and get to work. And remember, you don't really have to smoke it.

SURVIVING CHILDHOOD

....

This is for the young ones, who feel that life isn't fair, that you never get to do what you want or have any say. I'm speaking to all those little guys and gals out there who are forced to endure life without freedom, without choices and with no escape. Your parents won't say it but I will—you are being held hostage.

Your kidnappers may not be evildoers; they probably have good intentions. But let's be clear—you are being held captive against your will. You have no independence, no money, no escape, and that is all by design. I should know, because I've been on both sides. I was once a hostage and I am now holding a couple hostages myself, and I'm here to help.

Right now, bedtime, mealtime, playtime are all according to your parents' schedule. They drop plans on you as if you had none of your own. They walk into your room without knocking and tell you to get in the car.

"Where are we going?" you ask.

"I said, Get. In. The. Car."

It's a wonder they don't blindfold you. You figure out from nothing but clues that they're taking you to your aunt's house—and not the good aunt's house.

"Give her a kiss."

You hesitate. Of course you hesitate.

"Now."

Well, this wasn't what you had planned for today. You had important things to do. You were going to go outside and stuff. Did they even consider that? No, they did not. Do they consider that you won't enjoy spending the afternoon in an old woman's house that smells like a dusty bookcase? No, and not only do they not care, they'll tell you how you are supposed to feel about it.

"That was fun—you love going to see your aunt."

How can they even say that? What part of going to a place with no toys, games or young people do they think will be fun? Staring at the mole on her face and counting the hairs coming out of it? Trying not to get bitten by her nasty little dog? Or maybe they think you really like sitting on a hard chair and doing nothing but watching old people get older right before your eyes.

Why don't they just leave you at home? You would survive; you're not a baby. You know how to sit in your room and watch a show without lighting the house on fire. And why do they always think you're going to light things on fire? You don't smoke, have no interest in burning anything and have never given them any indication that you do. It's a leftover fear from centuries ago when people used lanterns for light and decorated their Christmas trees with candles.

No, the real reason they don't leave you behind is because

they're afraid you'll try to escape, and that, truth be told, is a valid concern. Haven't you ever gotten on your bike and thought about pedaling as fast and as far as you can? Who hasn't fantasized about the rest of your family . . . not dying exactly, but maybe getting caught in a tunnel or a well somewhere and not being able to come home for a month or two?

Don't feel bad about it: It's entirely natural. You wouldn't even have these creepy thoughts if they left you alone for a single afternoon while they go off and eat weird pumpernickel sandwiches with that woman they say is your aunt but who doesn't seem to be related to either of your parents.

Do you ever notice that when you go on these visits you hear the adults whispering behind your back when you leave the room? You're not paranoid—they are totally talking about you. They know you are keeping things from them but they can't figure out what they are. Good for you. Keep those secrets. You need to develop your own personality, and if you tell them everything they will criticize everything and you'll end up just like them: worried about everything.

Here's something important that I learned in the eighth year of my prison sentence. As strong and powerful and rich as they are compared to you, you have something they don't. Youth. As soon as I understood that I was physically superior to my capturers, everything changed.

Think about it: You are more flexible than they are, giving you the ability to climb into small spaces that they can't go. You can see better than they do, which is the real reason they get so angry when they see you reading in the dark. Their eyes are so old and crusty that they need lamps everywhere they sit. And you have *way* more energy than they do. They need to sleep all the time, like bears in perpetual hibernation. Just look at them nodding off on the couch in the middle of the afternoon, passing out during movies and snoring on airplanes. They're exhausted. You can use that.

This makes sleepovers way more fun. All you have to do is wait for them to go to bed and you're free to do what you want. Trust me, they don't want to get up. There are times I hear noises that sound like an axe murderer roaming through my house and I stay in bed because although I want to protect my family, more than anything else I really want to sleep.

Your parents think they know every part of the house, and they may have a good sense of it, but, like a crafty rodent, it's your job to go where they can't. We had a crawl space in the basement. It was a raised concrete storage area that ran under half the house. My father used it to store Christmas decorations and other items that weren't used every day, but once he put enough things in there that went beyond his arm's reach he would send me in. I would have to crawl along the dusty concrete with a flashlight in my hand and retrieve whatever dumb thing he needed.

But one day, I found something more valuable than any old box of Easter decorations: I found space. There was a whole section of the crawl space that was unused because my father couldn't get back there. But I could, and now I had what every hostage needs and wants—a hideout. I could hide dirty magazines in there, I could hide snacks in there, I could hide myself in there, and that's exactly what I did for hours on end.

I'm sure you have a space like that too. Have a look around in the rear of a closet, under the carpet or behind some large piece of furniture. You are looking for a door or empty space small enough that the big people won't fit but big enough for you to create the perfect hideaway. Find it, get in there and don't leave a trail.

Money is a big part of your predicament. They say the reason children can't work before the age of sixteen is that the adults are protecting you and ensuring that you aren't exploited, but the truth is they don't want you to have a job because they don't want you opening a bank account, applying for a credit card and getting your own apartment. Money equals freedom, and they don't want you to have any. So steal it.

Sure, it might be wrong, but so is holding a child in poverty for almost two decades. Nelson Mandela broke the law. So did MLK, Elvis and Jane Goodall. Sometimes we have no choice but to break the rules and tell The Man he can't push you around. This is one of those times, and your parents are The Man.

You don't want to get caught, so you have to be as crafty as the mouse that you are, and for that reason I am going to advise you to only steal change. Coins are a dirty, archaic form of currency that will be phased out eventually, and everybody feels it coming, which is why no one picks them up when they drop them or notices when any of them are missing. Gather them up in all the places people leave them: cupholders, that stupid junk drawer, under couch cushions and in and around every car.

And here's another tip: Your kidnappers are so annoyed by coins that if you simply ask, the minute they get some they will gladly give them to you. It seems like nothing to them, but in no time at all, if you are a dedicated pirate, you will have an impressive treasure chest tucked in the back of the crawl space you call home.

So now you have some money, and you have some space—but don't jump the gun. You have to be patient and play along. The one thing you don't want to do is freak them out with outlandish behavior. If your kidnappers get nervous, they will clamp down even harder and take away even more of your rights. You have to suck it up, do as they say, play their little game and be patient.

When they tell you that you can't wear something that you want to wear, go change. Trust me—it's not worth the fight, and it's one of the first things they look for when you are acting out. From ages five to ten I was dressed like a seventies porn star. Was I comfortable? No. Did I look good? No. I looked like a tiny pimp or a used-car salesman from Alabama, but I certainly didn't look like anyone else in my class.

This was because the warden in my penitentiary, my mother, with no training at all as a fashion designer, was in charge of my wardrobe. I was forced into plaid pants that would have been offensive for a couch in the basement of a frat house. I was given three types of shirts to choose from: polyester, turtlenecks and so-tight-they-made-me-look-like-a-fat-sausage.

And the hair. I had bangs. This was the only style my hairdresser—who, incidentally, was again my mother—could cut. I had bangs, plaid pants and chunky suede shoes. I looked like a hipster barista girl from Vassar College, but I was a boy living in New Jersey and going to East Brook Elementary.

Was this torture? You bet it was. At the very least it was thoughtless. I can understand just grabbing whatever when you're shopping. What kind of paper plate? Whatever. What kind of toilet paper? Whatever. What kind of dish towel? Whatever. But what type of clothing you are going to dress your child in as he tries to win friends and navigate his way through the social minefield of school should require a little thought.

Or maybe she *had* thought about it and this was her way of stopping me from running away. If you dress a chubby kid in a lady's sweater-vest and clogs, odds are he won't get any farther than the bus station.

We argued about it every morning, but I lost every time. I did manage a work-around where I would stash one of my favorite T-shirts into my lunch box and change halfway to school. I would run behind a tree, strip down and look cool in a matter of minutes. If you do this, don't make the mistake I made and show up in your T-shirt during picture day, then a couple months later watch as your mom receives the pictures she ordered, opens the envelope and sees you posing with a big smile in your favorite Led Zeppelin T-shirt.

You are not alone. You are not crazy. You know what freedom looks like and you know you're not living it. But remember—the one thing your parents can't do is stop the clock. Eventually you will be old enough to move out and start your own life and they won't be able to do a thing about it.

So until then, be respectful and courteous and steal as much money as you can.

WHY WE RETURN TO THE SEA

....

Humankind has been answering the call to the sea from the very first time our ancestors dreamed of a sweet shrimp cocktail. Maybe it's because we are mostly water and feel the connection between the tides and our pulsing hearts. Maybe we are returning to the ocean because we evolved from primitive fish people. Or maybe we're just hungry.

The Vikings developed long sea vessels that navigated the oceans and changed the course of European history. Asia used the seas to navigate new trade routes that connected the wealth and knowledge of all humankind. And my family rented a tiny motorboat at the Jersey Shore and puttered out onto the Barnegat Bay to see if we could catch some crabs.

We don't come from a long line of fishermen. The only boats in our origin story were the giant ships that brought us over from Italy and Germany after World War I, and those were far from majestic. My four-year-old grandfather was tossed around in the bottom of a giant metal hull surrounded by hundreds of desperate immigrants and was allowed to come up to the deck once a day, to throw up over the side. For years afterward he would get seasick just thinking about water. If they ever sing a sea shanty about my family's adventures, it will be called "They Had Inner-Ear Problems."

I would love to say that our decision to find a boat and head out on the bay had something to do with our ancient Sicilian heritage, but it was actually a painted sign we could see from the causeway that read "Go Crabbing! Boat Rental $5 an Hour."

We had headed down the Garden State Parkway on a vacation to where New Jersey met the sea. There, we would float around on rafts with mouthfuls of fudge and taffy as the ocean knocked us over and spit us back onto the shore. But although we knew nothing about the sea other than the five feet below our chins, something about that sign called out to us, and my father decided we should rent a boat.

We had never gone crabbing. We had never eaten crabs. Crabs were the mysterious creatures that ruined a nice swim in the ocean by biting our toes. But the price was right, and before we knew it we were renting gear and buying bait, and—like many of the other unfortunate fish in the sea—we were hooked.

Our first trips were more like silent-film comedies than fishing excursions. There were a lot of anchors lost, fishing hooks stuck in our shirts and lines that caught nothing but seaweed. We were learning, which is always humbling, but with practice, very little patience and my father's yelling, we started to make our way. Crabbing isn't exactly difficult. It's a lot like fly-fishing for people who are too stupid to fly-fish.

On our most successful early trip, we pulled into the dock with a bucket of six crabs and a lot of pride, only to be put in our place when we eyed the bushels of crabs that were unloaded on the docks by the more experienced. When my father realized how paltry our take was, he made my sister pour them back into the bay. But we were determined.

There were two different methods that we went with—trapping and netting. The traps were essentially metal wire boxes that were tossed overboard and then opened up wide when they hit the bottom. The four sides were tied off with string into one main line. The idea was that the crab would walk in and nibble on the bait, and when it was time to check the trap, we'd pull up the string, the sides would close and any crab that was in there would be trapped. We'd open one side, slide the crab into a bucket, check if the bait needed changing, toss it back into the bay and sit and wait again.

The netting method was more exciting. We'd tie a piece of bunker baitfish to the end of a weighted string, toss it off the side of the boat and dangle it just enough to entice a crab to come and take a bite. Once there was a tug on the line you had to slowly bring the line back to the surface—gently enough that the crab wouldn't realize what was happening and swim off. With the other hand you'd extend the pole with the attached net and come in from behind. Crabs swim backward, so if there was any attempt at escape they'd head right into the waiting net, then get flipped into the bucket and eventually into our bellies.

There is some finesse involved, which we developed over time along with other bits of wisdom, like don't toss a beer can into the water while your son is trying to quietly reel in a line and if you have to pee off the side of the boat, don't do it on the crab side.

We got pretty good at it over the years and started calling ourselves crabbers. Crabbers looking for Blue Point crabs from the Barnegat Bay. We started to go with enough regularity that all my father had to do was yell down the hall "We're going crabbing tomorrow" and my sisters and I would spring into action. We'd load the nets and traps into the car. We'd inspect the buckets for the essentials like string, weights and knives. And most of all we'd make sure there were snacks.

We all had our roles, and my father was the captain. Describing your father is a lot like trying to describe the Grand Canyon or the sky—there's so much there that eventually you end up lost in the vastness of it all. But one of my father's dominant traits is that he likes to be the boss. He was the boss at work, the boss at home and the boss of the boat. It was a small craft—no more than twelve feet long with three rows of benches—but every ship needs a captain, and he was it.

"I'll drive," he'd say. "You get the bait ready."

A good captain gets a lot of work out of his men, and one of my father's most cunning strategies was making me feel like I was valuable and needed. I was the oldest child and the only boy, and this position led to my doing a lot of things, like sweeping the garage, raking leaves, shoveling snow and, when on the water, cutting open fish heads and running a string through their eye sockets to create a treat that would be attractive to a hungry crab.

As I did the important work of preparing the lines in the front of the boat, my father guided the outboard motor from his position in the back. My sisters sat in the middle of the boat on a bench like mermaids taking a break, squinting straight ahead in matching life preservers, their curly hair bouncing in the wind like synchronized tufts of seaweed as the boat slammed its way across the water.

Once the captain picked out a lucky spot, he'd cut the engine, my sisters' hair would come to a rest and I'd toss out the anchor.

I'd stand at the head of the boat; I think they call it the "starboard," or maybe the "aft." I never learned the term—I'd just respond to my father yelling, "Get up there and throw the damn thing."

This went on for several throws at least, until the anchor caught on the bottom, we were steady and it was time.

"Let's crab!"

We'd set out our lines and drop the traps, each sister reaching over her side of the boat, and if we were getting some bites we would stay. If not, my father would get impatient and we would change our location.

"I'm not feeling it. This isn't a lucky spot," he'd say.

There was no GPS involved. No reading of tide maps. This entire venture was dependent on luck. Sometimes we had it and sometimes we didn't. If we ended up with a lucky day, the next time out we would try to replicate it with a series of superstitions—What type of knot did we tie? Which way was the boat facing? What did we have for breakfast?

On bad days we'd move every five minutes, tempers flaring, half-eaten bait thrown at the gods. But on good days the buckets would fill up pretty quickly and we'd have time to enjoy ourselves, drinking Pepsi and eating our homemade sandwiches in the summer sun. Our cooler was packed with ham and cheese or turkey and cheese on white bread wrapped in tinfoil, and if it sat around long enough the cheese would begin to melt in a really great way. My father would drink cans of Budweiser and if we ran out of soda I might get a sip or two.

At the end of a successful haul, after the bait had been cut loose and the salt water and beer had done its work on my father, I'd get my shot to drive us back to port. It was the same as starting up the lawn mower at home, when I'd put my sneaker on the green outer edge of the Lawn-Boy for leverage, grab hold of the rubber handle and yank at the rope as hard as I could. Every misfire made me feel foolish, but as soon as she came to life I would stand upright and wipe my brow in triumph as if the connection between a teenager's arm, a piece of rope and a small engine was somehow a confirmation that man can truly control the world.

As a teenage boy, being on the water gave me a unique sense of freedom. Nowhere else could I have a beer at my side and a vehicle under my control. There is a sense of lawlessness on the high seas, which is attractive to the likes of riverboat casinos, pillaging pirates and young men who aren't allowed to drive on land yet.

My father would bark out directions: "Aim for that bridge. Stay to the left of that boat. Watch the wake, for Christ's sake."

Every once in a while the throttle would slip out of my hand and the boat would lurch. My sisters would turn and eyeball me from their perch to make sure I wasn't losing it. I'd give them a "What are you looking at?" older brother stare. They'd look at each other to see if they should be concerned and, once satisfied, return to squinting at the horizon like two cranky cruise line guests.

Why? Why embark on an all-day journey pushed by this tiny motor and in this small boat in order to try to catch some crabs that we could have bought at the local fishery for under twenty dollars? Because of course it wasn't about the crabs, it was about the time together.

Some families spend time together playing tennis or golf or sitting poolside at the country club. Our time was shared on a boat, on the bay, sharing a ham and cheese sandwich while covered in salt water, sharing a laugh because that just didn't happen on land.

This went on for years, and slowly, without planning or anticipating, we actually started to truly understand the sea. We became aware of the subtle changes in the days. We learned that a wind kicking up from the east would bring with it the dreaded greenhead horseflies. We could tell which way the tide was moving by the way our lines drifted on the surface. We knew, in the way a seafaring family would, how to tell the time by the sun's position in the sky, give or take an hour or two.

We understood the rhythm of the seasons. June was a little too early. August brought a humid, heavy stillness, creating a waveless bay with a glassy surface that was as quiet and soundless as it was unmoving. The season ended in late September, when we started catching mostly pregnant crabs, which we returned to the water not because we were good people but because we knew that meant there would be more crabs to catch next season.

As the years went on and my sisters got bored and drifted toward the ocean to sunbathe with our mother, my father and I continued on our own. We had become salty veterans of the bay who no longer needed all that equipment and extra lines from our early harebrained days. We were crabbing on pure instinct. There were no more beers and no more tinfoil sandwiches. We even got to the point that we no longer used bait or even a boat. All we needed was our nets and our crab-altered brains.

During my high school years, we would walk down to the end of our street onto a sandy path that cut through a thicket of tall reeds. We'd emerge at the water's edge, set a bucket on the shore and wade into the bay with our nets at the ready. The water was so clear we could see our way around the beds of seaweed as we searched for the crabs hiding underneath, resting nearby or swimming through. If we spotted one, in an act of controlled stillness we'd slowly move the net into the water and scoop up the critters.

In a way, we were honoring the mighty crustacean by lessening our impact on its environment. I'd imagine myself as an early native who, although dressed in a bathing suit and football jersey, knew how to move silently in concert with the nature around me. We were now a part of the water and the tide and the wind and the setting sun.

Our crabbing journey ended toward the end of the last season before I headed off for college. In those final days, we waded through the water mostly in silence, except for my father's occasional bit of advice or question about my readiness.

Changes were coming and we both knew that this moment wouldn't last. He was no longer the boss, and I would soon be leaving for good. But for one last time, we remained as just a dad and his kid. It was perfect, but it couldn't stay that way.

The sea doesn't work like that.

THERE'S NO CURE FOR A HANGOVER

....

A benefit of drinking too much is waking up the next day and being forced to evaluate the choices you've made, not just from the night before, but since the day you were born. It is a necessary purging of your ego that can be as cleansing as it is painful, and it can only occur when you're in a really bad way. If this sounds like something uncomfortable that you'd rather avoid, then order an herbal tea and get to bed early. However, if you're open to an honest assessment of how you're living, bottoms up and enjoy the night.

Recently, we celebrated a good friend's fiftieth birthday. I started with two beers, moved on to two healthy vodka martinis with six jumbo olives and followed up with several pitchers of cheerful sangria, which I begrudgingly shared with friends. This led to late-night shots and the mauling of an entire key lime pie with a spoon.

Once safely home, I stumbled around in the dark, drinking out of the bathroom sink, trying to hydrate. But nothing good ever comes from a bathroom sink. I don't know if the water is really that different from the kitchen faucet, but it sure feels that way, which is probably why 90 percent of bathroom sink water is swished around with toothpaste and spit right back out.

When the sun came up through the window that I forgot to close, I took a deep breath and realized to my surprise that I wasn't hungover. That was because I was still drunk. I knew I must be drunk because I actually thought I felt good enough to get on the bike or go for a run. Why not get in some early morning exercise?

I've always secretly wanted to be one of those people. They seem like winners because nothing stops them. But I am not one of those people. I'm more like the people who roll over and go back to sleep, which is what I did that morning, and when I awoke a few hours later I was properly hungover and definitely not a winner.

The extent of a hangover will vary depending on what you drank, how much you mixed and, more than anything else, your age. The younger you are the more you can drink and the shorter the hangover will be. When you're older you can drink far less and yet your hangover will last much longer. I've had hangovers that have lasted so long they turn into an illness that lingers for weeks, making it tough to even remember that the whole ordeal started with drinking. It doesn't help that around this time your memory is starting to go.

Human beings have dealt with hangovers for centuries. Every solution is useless, which of course doesn't stop people from telling you what you need to do. It's the same as the many futile suggestions for fighting the common cold, like hot tea with lemon, zinc gummies and wearing big wool socks to bed. And although none of these methods prevent anyone from getting sick, everyone desperately wants you to try them. At least they care.

A popular bit of hangover advice is that you need "a little hair of the dog that bit you," which simply means drinking more. That's not a cure, that's extending your bad behavior, taking a nap and feeling slightly less damaged than you did before. Other techniques involve egg sandwiches, greasy foods and gallons of Gatorade. Some weirder ones include ancient roots from Chinatown, praying to God and taking fizzy tablets that you can only get in Europe. All of them are good at only one thing: creating the illusion that we are doing something to feel better, when all we can really do is wait for time to pass and try not to feel bad about feeling bad.

My only minor attempt at a cure on this foggy morning was a cup of black coffee that was a lot more difficult to make than it should have been. After many regrettable mistakes, I stood in the kitchen holding on to an overly bright Hello Kitty coffee mug as if it contained a magical potion, but when the caffeine started to kick in I only felt worse. Something was wrong. I wasn't sure if something bad had happened or was about to happen, but either way I was acutely aware that there was an unsettling ripple in the universe, and it had nothing to do with what was in my cup.

In search of the cause of my angst, I lay flat on the kitchen floor and started sorting through an itemized list of my mistakes. I started off with scorned lovers and closed bank accounts. There were mistakes from kindergarten, a thing that happened in gym class and most of what happened in high school. I thought about how fat I am, how old I've gotten and what little hair I have left on my head. I thought about all I haven't accomplished, all the people I've let down and all the times I didn't exercise. All my shortcomings were dredged up and strung together like skywriting in order to tell the whole world that it had finally been confirmed—I'm a loser.

I tried to defend myself from myself, but I was defenseless. And as I finished the first cup of coffee my self-loathing and insecurity dialed in one more immediate and unanswerable question: What did I do wrong last night?

At this age it's rarely a case of trying to remember what I did, but rather what I said. When I was younger and had good knees, I was known to get drunk and do outrageous things. I would put my finger out through the fly of my jeans in what I thought was a hilarious and original bit that quickly became my trademark. I once snuck into a utility room at college and flipped a giant electrical switch that turned off power to half the campus. I accidentally lit a dumpster on fire outside our dorm rooms and hid in my bed and watched as a city fire truck came to put it out. I wasn't just drunk, I was reckless, and relentlessly going for as big a laugh as I could get.

When I would wake up the next day, slowly realizing what I had done, I was rarely upset with myself. There was the occasional regret and apology, but I was young, stupid and mostly just a problem to myself. I never got into drunken fights or drove anything more dangerous than a bicycle. I did have some overly dramatic, tear-filled arguments with a girlfriend or two, but those were just scenes written for our own private opera.

Today the most regrettable act usually involves saying something offensive. Did I go overboard trying to make a point and insult someone? Did I profess my love for the wrong person? Did I try out my new Spanish and get it wrong?

The best way to figure out what, if anything, went wrong is to check in with my wife. I won't come out and ask directly as much as circle around, pass her in the hallway or quietly enter the kitchen and evaluate her mood from a safe distance. I'll start with a small smile and hope for the best. If she smiles back, I'm good. If she smiles back and shakes her head, I may have done something wrong but—thankfully—not to her. If she doesn't respond with any warmth, she most likely won't come out and say what I did right away, but it will definitely reveal itself before breakfast is over.

This particular morning she smiled back. I thought I was in the clear. Truly, beyond saying something stupid to my wife I don't really care, and I was pretty sure that last night was error-free, although I did remember a really big laugh but, sadly, couldn't remember the joke I'd told.

The clearest thing I could remember was the key lime pie. If the pie was the highlight of the night, I figured we were in pretty good shape. It was a fun night with a lot of good humor and good people, and my recent avoidance of the news had given me a lot less to be angry about. (It turns out not giving a shit is a great strategy for a happy life.)

"You owe Lisa an apology," said my wife.

"Uh-oh," I thought.

"Me?" I said.

"You know she wasn't feeling great about turning fifty. What were you thinking?"

"I was kidding," I said, not knowing what she was talking about but pulling out my go-to excuse.

She left the room. I may have been safe from her, but not from my own thoughts. I went off and tried to piece things together. What exactly did I say? It was all a bit of a boozy haze.

I remembered getting to the party and popping open those early beers, but then it was nothing but gaps filled with bits and pieces: an onion dip, a guy with a handlebar mustache, a dog swimming in the pool, someone yelling "Sangria," a chugging contest, a debate about flying squirrels, my wife taking a hot dog out of my hand and then . . .

Oh yeah. It slowly came back. Apparently, I had gone up to the birthday girl and said, "Happy fiftieth. Aren't you glad that you don't have to worry about what you look like anymore?"

It was a joke. I thought it was funny. I'm laughing now. Lisa was crying.

At this point the Advil proved useless, bouncing off my headache like a housefly against a window. The bad behavior now confirmed, the self-analysis began. Maybe I'm not as nice as I think I am. And maybe hiding behind jokes all the time is a cowardly act. Why did I say that? It's her birthday. She's trying to be happy. That's the point of "Happy Birthday." She didn't ask for a man in an ill-fitting Hawaiian shirt to walk up and tell her she's old and ugly.

I was grabbing myself by the collar and letting myself have it. I dug in and started questioning everything. Seriously, what am I doing with my life? Why do I turn everything into jokes? But then I rallied. I fought it off. So what if I turn tragedy into jokes? Some people turn it into sorrow. Some turn it into a noose that they hang themselves with. At least I'm trying to turn it all into something that we can laugh at so we can carry on.

But when that joke is directed toward a friend who's turning fifty, maybe I'm just an asshole.

I heard my wife approaching. This was not a good sign. This had nothing to do with Lisa. She hadn't seemed too angry before, but now the cues that only a married partner would notice were ringing loudly off the back of my skull. There was a new development, but I had no idea what it was.

"You don't even remember, do you?" said my wife.

"Remember what?" I was forced to ask that horrible question.

"You have no idea what you did or how much you have embarrassed me?"

All I could do was wince and shake my head no.

She held up her phone. It was a picture, part of a group text with what looked like twelve people. And there I was, a big smile on my face, holding a pineapple drink in one hand while one of my fingers was peeking out of my pants.

My wife and the accompanying hangover were really forcing me to look at myself and evaluate not only what I did but what I have become. Here was photographic proof that I have grown into a man who hasn't grown at all and still thinks that making rude, drunken gestures in public is somehow funny.

But honestly, in a moronic, trying-to-have-a-good-time-at-a-boring-party kind of way, I think it is pretty funny, and I told her so.

"Yeah, well you didn't have to chase Lisa with it."

Huh. I don't remember that part. That's definitely not funny at all. Or is it?

HOW YOU KNOW WHEN IT'S TIME TO GO

Small-town living has always appealed to me, and for a while I really tried to live it. I pushed aside any youthful ideas of moving away and doing great things and instead rented an apartment a few miles from where I went to high school. I got a job in a small local ad agency. I bought some cheap suits from Macy's and wrote ad copy about the joyous benefits of moving your loved ones into the Shady Lane Nursing Home for their final days. It was a strange thing to write about at the invincible age of twenty-two, but I didn't care—it was a stable job and I was happy to have it.

I dated an average local gal, but in New Jersey at our favorite dive bar she looked like a movie star. If she'd been famous they would've written articles about how her crooked tooth and lazy eye added to her charm in a quirky girl-next-door kind of way. I didn't care that her nose looked like it belonged on a much bigger face, I thought she was great—and to be honest, a little out of my league.

I had long curly hair that was an inch away from being a mullet and weighed about thirty pounds more than I do right now, and I'm currently ten pounds overweight. I didn't know how to dress or what to wear, but at that time Bruce Springsteen looked good in a leather vest so I wore one too, only mine was made of cheap felt, so I didn't look like The Boss as much as I looked like an amateur magician on his way to get new headshots.

My friends were the kids from high school who in some unspoken pact decided not to move away like our classmates but instead saw the good in sticking around. We had become the next generation of "locals," and we drank beers with the older locals at a bar called The Library, whose name made us feel like we were doing something smart. But we were people who got drunk and threw darts at the busboy, not people who were there to read books. We lived for the end of the week, because it meant more money and less work and we could drink more heavily than we did on Thursday or sometimes on Wednesday and once in a while on Tuesday.

We gorged ourselves on bar food, late-night pizza and the royal offerings from the Dairy Queen and the Burger King. We were fat and happy, and it seemed like we could have gone on like this for at least as long as our hearts held out, which you knew wasn't necessarily very long if you kept an eye on the local obituaries. We all started to look the same, like round, puffy-faced volunteer firemen who stood by in my apartment waiting for the alarm to sound so we could rush out and risk our lives for a little excitement.

My girlfriend and I shared a place on the second floor of a large green two-story family home that overlooked the Garden

State Parkway. It was a highway that didn't allow trucks, so it wasn't so loud and I actually enjoyed watching the cars go by, especially when there was traffic. While I was on the phone, which was attached to the wall, I would gaze out the window through the pantry and think how smart I was to be inside munching on Oreos while those poor bastards were killing themselves trying to get home.

Our landlords were an Italian family, parents and two sons about our age, who lived underneath us on the first floor. They were very nice, kind of kooky and seemed to yell more than speak, and we would often test their patience with late-night parties, loud wrestling matches and all the annoying things that young adults engage in. They tolerated a lot from us, until we annoyed them way too much, way too late, which would cause them to bang on the door and stare at me in disbelief.

This was the home base where we would start and end the night if we were heading out to the bars, or where we would hang out if we were staying in. The door was always open, and many days I'd come home from work and find the party had already started. My living room would be filled with friends yelling and screaming through a cloud of marijuana smoke, playing NHL Hockey on Sega Genesis.

This early video game took over our lives for a good year. We played relentlessly, with tournaments that went on day and night. No one was working toward a career as much as clocking hours at a job, so as soon as it was quitting time it was a race to the apartment, where we could get back to the important parts of our lives—doing bong hits, grabbing the controllers and battling for the cherished Stanley Cup. It was a replica of the real thing crafted out of aluminum foil and a toilet paper roll, and we fought as hard to win it as anyone in the NHL.

We had very little money and no goals, which gave us a sense of contentment that only the semiretired enjoy. I knew I was wasting time, but a part of me liked the simplicity. Each week was the same—work, party and go to an infinite number of family birthday parties and holiday get-togethers whose only variation was which couch you'd be sitting on this time. No thought, very little risk and lots of cake.

I wasn't thinking about anything more than having a good time, and while I would secretly daydream of a bigger, more determined life, I truly enjoyed the calming effect of being surrounded by the familiar.

It was on these streets that as a child I could close my eyes in the backseat and know exactly where we were. I knew the feel of the off-ramp, the big bump in the road and the last left that took us up Kenwood Drive, where my father would cut the engine as we silently coasted back home into the driveway and parked under the leaning birch tree.

I learned that the gas station light stayed on long after they'd closed, that the lake froze in the winter and became stagnant and still in the summer. I knew the smell of the giant oak leaves fermenting on the sidewalks and what it all felt like after a long hard rain. This is what it means to be home, to really know a place, to feel safe and wanted. But those same places sometimes have a natural way of pushing us out.

During the New Jersey winters, as we were forced to turn inward, away from the constantly gray skies and wet, muddy roads, a certain bleakness would take hold. We'd wear the same sweaters for months and get even fatter, and while there were some cozy nights, it was impossible to not feel like something was wrong or at the very least that there was something else we should have been doing.

The thing about living in New Jersey is that you can literally see a bigger, more exciting life right across the Hudson River. The entire New York City skyline was the teasing backdrop of my young adult life. It was just a quick ride over a bridge or through a tunnel to a world that couldn't have been more different from the one I was living in. For someone who was thinking about comedy and acting and writing, that skyline was almost laughing at me while I drove around in my Ford Escort to get another Butterfinger Blizzard. It's one thing to watch *Saturday Night Live* while you're living in Kansas; it has an entirely different effect when you can see the Empire State Building blinking out your window.

But along with the allure, the city was something we feared. The city didn't open up and welcome you in—it dared you to make the trip. The way commuters would come off the train looking like they'd been to war gave all of us pause. Saying that you were going into the city wasn't a casual statement, but a battle cry that meant that you'd better get prepared because bad things happen there and they'd probably happen to you.

We were warned about taking the bus and getting attacked by all the perverts at the Port Authority bus station. From the way it was told, all you had to do was make one stop in the men's room and you'd be trapped forever performing sex acts for subway tokens.

This was all too much for me. I was barely getting by on the mean streets of Bergen County, so I was convinced that a trip to the city would surely end in kidnapping or death. My worries were confirmed the time my friend Jason and I went to an arcade below Times Square on Broadway. His parents had a place in the city and while they would go to work in the Garment District Jason would run wild around Manhattan.

He was a lot like a street kid, which at thirteen made him a very exciting pal.

He'd asked me to come along with him to the city for the day and I'd accepted, because I was sure that my parents would laugh at the idea and send me to my room. But in a moment of poor parenting, they agreed to the plan, and before I knew it I found myself in the backseat of an early morning commute to my imminent death.

But to my surprise, my fears quickly melted away. "The city" was exciting and loud and colorful in a way that was unknown to me. It was shocking to think that this madness was going on all summer long while I was back home jumping through a sprinkler. We ate slices of pizza, talked to teasing prostitutes and, the most fun of all, went to the arcade.

This was the *Pac-Man* era, and arcades had exploded all over the country. Naturally, the ones in Manhattan were a little funkier than most, with video games mixed in with boardwalk-style Skee-Ball and pinball machines where you had to get the ball in between a scantily clad lady's legs. While an arcade in New Jersey attracted nothing but kids, the New York arcade attracted a host of hustlers on their way into or out of jail.

In the arcade as in life, as soon as you run out of money you run out of fun, and I was broke. I wandered around taking in the sights and watching other people enjoy themselves. I couldn't believe my good fortune when a nice man came up and held out a handful of quarters and asked if I needed some more money. With no street sense at all, and a trusting nature, I saw this as the lucky break that I deserved. Maybe New York wasn't so scary after all. No one ever gave me free money back home, and here was a complete stranger dropping quarters into the game for me—and not only that, he seemed to really enjoy watching me play.

Jason eventually came over and saw me playing *Space Invaders* while my new adult friend leaned over my shoulder. Jason, who had been to this arcade before, quickly told me that we had to go, which upset my new friend, who seemed offended and then angry and then demanded that I pay him back. As he grabbed my arm, Jason shoved him and yelled, "Run!"

I knew it. I'd been sucked into the allure of the Big Apple and now innocent young Tommy was running for his life. I was trying not to cry as the man chased us for a few blocks while Jason yelled at him and told everyone within earshot that a child molester was following us. This made me even more upset. I thought he was going to beat us, but I had no idea he was going to molest us as well. What kind of devil's playground was this place?

As our perverted pursuer faded into the crowd, we ducked into the comfort of a souvenir shop, where my spirits were lifted as we bought a plastic Statue of Liberty whose top came off when you pulled the torch.

As scary as it was almost being bought and sold on the child arcade trafficking market, I knew New York was the place to be. I could either get there and be a part of it or shrink away and accept its role as the looming, mocking backdrop to my New Jersey life, telling the story of what I could have been.

This isn't a declaration of big-town living over small-town life. I love them both. I crave them both. It actually has been the nagging torture of my existence. I crave the simple and then do everything I can to make life more difficult.

My decision was made in a single moment. We were drinking ice-cold Budweisers at a picnic table in the middle of the winter. My friends were moronically trying to hit a stop sign with rocks. Whenever they connected, the metallic clang would cause them to howl like drunken primates. I looked at my girlfriend, and she was hunched over, hiding under the hood of her tattered down jacket trying to light her cigarette in the driving wind. It was getting dark and the cold was becoming unbearable and no one seemed to care. Everyone was happy. Except me. I knew then that it was time to go.

I didn't want to disappear into a life of drinking beer and doing shots of Jose Cuervo and eating a steady diet of Hot Pockets and onion rings. I didn't want to disappear while going nowhere.

So I left.

It took some time, but in the name of a career and a great adventure I broke up with the girl and left that barful of friends and that version of myself and went out into a world filled with movement and new beginnings and constant endings.

Roots were abandoned for the next stop, and while I tried to stake a claim in new places, they didn't grow as deeply as if I had stayed. That's the sacrifice of leaving. I will never run into a friend of a friend who will tell me the news about someone's dog having puppies. I won't sit in the diner in the early morning where the old waitress who knew me when I was young with curly hair teases me about my disappearing hairline.

Some of my friends are still there and have made wonderful lives, and in certain moments while I'm boarding a sad commuter flight to some place I've never been, or trying to sleep in a bad hotel where I can hear strangers snoring and farting through the walls, I'm jealous of those who stayed.

I do have fantasies that I'll be headed back in that general direction at a certain point. I have been daydreaming about working in a bagel shop at the beach for so long that I think it might actually be a goal. But while I continue the debate, it doesn't change the fact that every day I wake up looking for coffee and something to eat.

A day is a day and while some may be busier than others, they all end the same, with the sun going down while I putter around assessing how I did and what I'll do tomorrow. I worry, hope and dream and pray that everything will work out. And wherever I end up, I know at the very least there's a bakery nearby that has biscotti dipped in chocolate, and that's good enough for me.

SOME THINGS THAT CAN KILL US

....

Despite all the advancements we have made in medicine, safety helmets and Bubble Wrap, there are a lot of things out there that can still get ya. Some are new and some have been around forever, but with the right karate skills and pepper spray you have a chance to survive them all.

Here's a refresher on some of the dangers you may have forgotten about.

Pirates—They've raped and pillaged for centuries, surviving plagues, natural disasters and Peter Pan, and they're still out there. They're sailing across the great blue sea under the good old Jolly Roger, never showering, never paying taxes and never drinking rum out of anything but dirty broken bottles. They wait all year for you landlubbers to book a cruise, rent a Jet Ski or finally give that paddleboard a try, and when you do they tie you up, steal your Starbucks gift card and send you straight to Davy Jones's locker, which means the bottom of the sea, where you have very little chance of staying alive.

Manholes—These are holes in the street that utility workers use to go belowground and fix stuff. They are usually plugged up with manhole covers, but sometimes, after a long day, the workers forget to put the cover back on, leaving a hole that you can easily fall into if you're texting, daydreaming or acting like a cartoon character. I'm not sure what's down there, but I can only imagine that if you don't have the proper training it will probably kill you or at least ruin a nice pair of pants.

Lawn Darts, Badminton and Croquet—If there is any sign that inviting people into your yard is a bad idea, it's the popularity of these games. They're silly, old and not that much fun, but what else are you going to do when you run out of things to talk about? You're going to need activities, and you'd be wise to remember how incredibly dangerous they are.

Lawn darts go through so many people's hearts it's like they're trying to do it on purpose. Badminton is so boring that players stop trying to hit that stupid shuttlecock and start whacking each other in the face just for fun. And everyone knows that if a croquet mallet is found in the trunk of a car, on the pages of a murder mystery or within ten miles of a dead body, it was definitely used to kill somebody. Pull up a lounge chair, settle down and be careful out there.

Gluten—I really hate to talk about this one and thought we'd moved past it, but I overheard someone at the next table during lunch and you should just know that it's back and apparently more dangerous than anything you could ever imagine. You just don't get it.

Wolverines—Unlike werewolves, these are real, have really big teeth and I just saw one on the internet. I'm not sure where they live, but they don't look like a lot of fun and are just one in a long list of things out there in the dark, hiding behind trees, waiting to pounce on us, like mountain lions, cave crickets and townies. Porcupines, grifters and tax attorneys are also out there in the wild, so get your rabies shot, carry an EpiPen and wear fancy cologne—wolverines hate that.

Other People—They're everywhere. I was in the lounge at the Portland Airport and they were all around me. The teenage girl in flip-flops and a Princess Leia haircut eating chips and licking her fingers. The guy with a waffle hanging out of his mouth like it was a freshly caught salmon. The businesswoman dressed in Sunday business casual, casually sneezing into her hands and wiping it on her stretchy jeans. They're everywhere and, even after a global pandemic, their manners have not improved.

Public Wi-Fi—Trying to connect to Wi-Fi in public places is a living hell. I hear it's pretty great and easy in South Korea, but here there will be ads to watch, passwords you don't know and apps you do not have. When you finally sacrifice all you know and love for a couple of minutes online, you will most likely be sucked into the dark web, turned into digital currency and made into a meme of a missing person. Good luck, and have your credit card ready.

Jazz—Everyone likes a little jazz, until you run into a trumpet player who gets carried away and plays the same note over and over and over, again and again and again. I'm sure it must feel really good if you're a jazz cat vibing out on D-flat, but if you're forced to listen to this while doing the dishes there is a good chance you may try to end it all by drinking an entire bottle of Dawn dishwashing soap with a Brillo pad chaser. Or you can cleanse your palate and run back into the exquisitely soothing sounds of the master himself, Oscar Peterson.

Poison Ivy—This is the stuff that waits for you out in the

woods, usually where you least expect it: along a beautiful path, in a bucolic picnic spot or wherever you are outside. You hike along thinking you're enjoying the great outdoors, and a day later you're covered with blisters that pop and spread and plunge you into itchy madness. It probably won't kill you, but it will make you run back inside where you belong, safe from other natural killers like ticks, all sorts of spiders and the sun.

Snake Oil Salesmen—They may not travel around in the elaborate wooden carts of yesteryear, but now they have websites and advertising budgets that will razzle-dazzle you into buying their wares. They promise a healthy future and a better you, with improved relationships and whiter teeth, but don't be fooled. Feeling kind of depressed and achy is normal, and anyone who promises to take you well above or below that threshold should not be trusted, especially if they are a retired football player or sitcom star.

Sunburn—What do day drinking, pool parties and canoe trips have in common? They're all fun ways to end up with a life-threatening, unattractive, third-degree sunburn. The sun apparently hates us now, and no matter how carefully you apply that sunblock you will end up with a perfect handprint on your chest and a red gourd for a nose. But at least you'll smell like coconut and that's nice.

Laughter—There's a reason the term "dying from laughter" exists. It's a condition caused by so much joy and connection with others that you actually laugh so hard your head pops off. It originated back in the 1800s when people never smiled, never came out of the coal mines and never heard jokes. When something truly funny would happen, like a rich guy falling down a flight of stairs or someone crashing one of those silly, giant bicycles, they'd laugh so hard they would die.

But there are worse ways to go.

TRUST

....

The sloppy and misguided have a strategy when leaving Las Vegas: Drink as much as possible and then head directly to the airport for the red-eye flight home. It's a horrible plan that at best guarantees nausea and unsettled sleep on the plane and, more likely, missed flights and throwing up at the gate.

I, on the other hand, was forced into catching the same flight because after a full week of shows at the Tropicana Las Vegas, I was nearing a nervous breakdown. Vegas can be fun for a night or two, but anything more and the casinos start to do dangerous things to your soul.

As a young comedian I was hired to do two shows a night for seven nights in a row. While I was happy for the work, I quickly learned that I wasn't going to be treated anything like Sinatra and his Rat Pack pals. There was no limo from the airport, no presidential suite, not even my name on the marquee. The closest I came to seeing my name in lights was the sign that read "Comedy at the Trop," right underneath "The Best All You Can Eat Buffet on the Strip."

They let you know very clearly that you are just another nameless employee who won't be around for long. My room was no bigger than a closet, all incidentals charged to my credit card and we could only eat in the employee cafeteria, which is one of the saddest places on earth. The glitz and glamour of Vegas—the dancing waterfalls and sequin-covered showgirls—are nowhere to be found in the dark, sticky underground of the employee cafeteria.

I'd sit with my Jell-O and bowl of Captain Crunch as the elderly cocktail waitresses, with their sore stocking feet, would size me up through the haze of their cigarette smoke. I felt like a virgin in a seedy brothel. They'd tease me about my youth and innocence as their tired breasts rested on their trays like gamblers leaning over the edge of a craps table.

The rest of the cafeteria was filled with dealers, security guards and housekeepers, all in the itchy polyester uniforms that looked more like prison garb than hotel staff uniforms. Cardboard dangled from the air vent where someone had taped it in an attempt to aim the fresh air away from the exhaled cigarette smoke.

A stay in any hotel more than three nights and you start to see the tricks behind the illusions, and in Vegas it's even more evident. There are the constant lights, music and crowd noise coming from the slot machines that are arranged to slow you down and get you to play. Everything from the shows to the magicians are advertised with the promise of sex. Even the ad in the elevator for the buffet was shot through the silhouetted legs of a beautiful woman, as if she'd be waiting to have sex with you next to the pile of king crab legs.

Of course none of it is real, and we all know that, but you don't really feel it until you've been there for an entire week, at which time the fanciest Vegas hotels reveal themselves as nothing more than the vertical strip malls that they are.

To this day I don't gamble when I'm performing at a casino, mainly because I watched the headliner that week sitting at the video poker machine late into the night. He'd mail any money he won back to his family, which was a sad, grand gesture offset by the fact that he lost most nights.

When the final show was over, I grabbed the bag that I had stashed backstage and ran directly to my friend's car. He worked the lights in the showroom and knew all the shortcuts to the airport, which I needed if I had any chance of making my flight. He was a good guy working all the angles in Vegas and claimed to have a foolproof technique for winning at roulette, but his beat-up Honda Civic with the dirty stick shift said otherwise.

I dragged my bag out of his dirty trunk, thrilled to have made it in time and to finally head back home to New York, but when I got inside the airport I knew I was screwed. There were way too many confused and sweaty humans for anything to be going right.

This was before smartphones, so there were no alerts and no warnings—you just showed up places and dealt with whatever was happening. Apparently a big storm was devouring the East Coast and causing delays all the way to Nevada. The line was longer than the DMV and customs lines combined.

After a long, confused walk, guided by people pointing behind them, I finally found the end of the line. I met a girl about my age who looked like a student carrying nothing more than a backpack.

"Have you heard anything?" I asked.

"Nothing."

"How long have you been here?"

"About an hour."

"That's not good."

"No it's not."

She was patient and quietly funny with a teasing smile, and together we tried to make sense of the chaos that was building around us. In moments like this you need a partner, someone to keep your place in line, hold your bag, bounce ideas off of, so without discussion we teamed up.

I made my way through the crowd, eavesdropping on conversations, trying to get some information from the adults yelling at the ticket counter. I heard someone yell, "I knew it. You couldn't have canceled it two hours ago?"

I ran back to my friend and told her the bad news, that we wouldn't be flying until the morning.

"Now what do we do?" I asked.

"I don't know. Go back to our hotels?"

That hadn't occurred to me; technically I still had a room, but I didn't want to go back to the Tropicana. I didn't want to see that hotel ever again.

After figuring out our escape plans, it felt like we should have stuck together, but we went our separate ways, joking that we would see each other in a few hours and that hopefully the line would be shorter then. She may have gone back to her hotel. I slept outside a closed Nathan's hot dog stand.

Her name was Pam, and it was one of those chance meetings when you just feel an instant comfort with someone. I'm sure it could be explained away as the result of the exhaustion from the week or the euphoria that it was over, but I instantly liked her, without any flirtation or motive. I really just needed a friend, and we were two kids who met at the playground and instantly ran off to the swings together.

I didn't see her in the morning when I finally got on the flight. I was hoping that she made it and that she was all right. I craned my neck from the back of the plane and saw what I thought could have been her up ahead, but I wasn't sure. It wasn't until the captain came on, hours into our trip, to tell us that the New York airports were closed and that we had been rerouted to Columbus, Ohio, that she turned around and rolled her eyes at me. She knew I had been there all along.

I instantly felt relieved that although I'd be landing somewhere in Ohio, I wasn't alone. Our adventure continued.

She waited for me as we disembarked.

"What have you heard?" I asked.

"We may get out tonight, but they won't know for a while."

"Hmm. To the bar?"

"To the bar!"

She was going to college somewhere in Pennsylvania. She played softball and liked the school. She was headed back home to see her family for one last stop during her spring break. We had a couple of beers and struck up conversations with the other people at the bar, most of them in the same limbo we were in.

I love when a group of strangers at a bar form an instant community. There were the businessmen who were missing their meetings. The loud guy who was funny enough to not be annoying. The older couple who weren't troubled by the delay at all, as if waiting here was just the same as being at home on the couch together. Once in a while a scout would come back with a travel update. It was becoming clear that there was very little chance we would be getting out of there that night.

We overheard one of the experienced travelers say it would probably be smart to start looking for a place to stay. He was right. Everything was booked. We had very little money, no apps—no cell phones!—or any connection to the town we were now stranded in. It looked like my new friend and I might be sleeping in the airport, which didn't have as many options as Vegas. But just as we were losing hope, one last call from the pay phone revealed a Holiday Inn that had one room left. I booked it immediately, hung up and Pam and I looked at each other as if we needed to assess the plan we had set in motion but hadn't talked through yet.

"One room?" she asked.

"Yeah."

"Two beds?"

"I think so."

"Umm . . ."

"We should split it."

"I don't have any money."

"No, not that. I mean the room. We can totally do it. We've come this far. It would be weirder if we didn't."

She thought for a minute.

"Okay. I think you're right."

I assured her that it would be safe, that sharing a room with a wayward comedian from New York might seem like an unusual thing to do, but that this was an unusual day and I wasn't a creep so the odds of something weird happening were cut in half.

"Are you saying that *I* might attack *you*?" she asked.

"Yes. But it's a risk I'm willing to take."

People don't hitchhike much anymore. What a quaint idea from what seems like a very distant time—hiking, but hitching rides along the way from strangers who are willing to help you out. Who knows, it might be just as safe today, but no one feels that way. They certainly didn't in the early 2000s, but Pam and I were unafraid. By sharing a room we were essentially jumping into a fur-lined van with a total stranger, but our instincts told us everything was going to be okay. We trusted each other completely.

The hotel room was your average clean, good-enough type of room designed for the weary. Places like this aren't final destinations but way stations that fill up at night and empty out in the early morning before the sun comes up. This was a pit stop, not a vacation spot.

We had a fun night filled with TV and salty snacks. We each took quick, stealthy showers and made our own nests on separate beds. We had a 7 A.M. flight and needed sleep, but after two extra nights on the road, a couple of beers and very little food we turned into kids at a sleepover party. Every time we tried to be quiet one of us would start giggling until we finally erupted into an all-out laughing fit. The absurdity of what we were doing—making this crazy leap of faith with someone we'd met in a Vegas airport—was downright hilarious.

In moments like this I try to evaluate the situation through the eyes of those who know me best. What would my father, sister or girlfriend say? Pam and I agreed that our friends and family would think we were nuts, but we knew better. As unlikely as it seemed, drifting off to sleep to the sound of her shallow breathing in the dark didn't feel foreign at all.

We were sitting pretty far apart on the plane, so we said our goodbyes as we boarded with a small laugh and a quick hug, the first time we'd touched during our adventure. After two long days, like pioneers, we finally made it across the country to Newark Airport. I didn't see her after we landed, but I did see her once again in New York about a year later. She came to one of my shows and introduced me to her sister as "This is the guy I told you about."

"Okay, now I can see it," her sister said. "But still . . ."

There are times on the road when I'm alone making my way alongside other weary travelers and I'll think about Pam and how special she was. I recently helped an older woman get her bag down from the overhead bin, and she thanked me and made a little joke. She was nice and all, but there was no way I was sharing a room with her. There was just something about her that I didn't trust.

A WISE ANCESTOR CALLED GRANDPA

....

Sometimes, in the search for lessons from our ancestors, all we have to do is pay attention to the people who show up for Thanksgiving. Every now and then there will be a pearl of wisdom dropped somewhere between the mashed potatoes and the green beans. The wise old sage at our family gatherings was often my grandfather, who taught me many things, mostly while not meaning to, sometimes while yelling at the TV and occasionally while muttering in his sleep as he napped on the couch.

He taught me that you can make a screwdriver out of a butter knife, a butter knife out of the handle of a hammer and a hammer out of a cast-iron skillet. He spent more time cobbling together tools than he did actually fixing things with them. There's a saying that you need to have the right tool for the job—and he never did. It seemed to me that the way he got any of it to work was by yelling "Shit" over and over again.

Grandpa's toolbox was really an oily shoebox, and anytime he needed to fix something he just rummaged through it, grabbed an instrument of destruction and did his best. His work area in the basement was an assortment of coffee cans and old cigar boxes filled with reused string, washers and bolts from old jobs and hundreds of keys to doors and locks that no longer existed.

He was a self-declared inventor. He looked at a world that didn't make sense and thought there had to be a better way and that he and his shoebox could find it. The invention he was most proud of was a small wire attachment that would keep the cap of the toothpaste attached to the tube.

"You know how you unscrew the cap and it flies off behind the toilet and you never see it again?" he'd ask.

"Uh-huh." I didn't really brush my teeth much in those days, but I was trying to be encouraging.

"Well, I'm going to fix that!"

I'd never known an inventor before, and here I had a grandpa who was one. I tried my best to follow in his confused footsteps. My parents say the first time they heard me swear, I was a small child with a plastic hammer imitating my grandfather. I walked around the house hitting things and yelling "Shit," the way I was taught.

His problem-solving wasn't calm and measured. It was an emotional response to what he saw as chaos. A way of working that I have unwillingly adopted. If something needs to be fixed in my house, I start off by playing a game of "Where Is It?": "Where's the screwdriver? Where is it? Has anyone seen it? Who used it last? Where is it? What's wrong with you people? Who stole the goddamn screwdriver? Why can't anyone put anything back where it belongs? Where? Is? It?" I run through the house opening drawers and cabinets, yelling at everyone, even if they're not there.

"Oh, here it is. Never mind, it was in my bathroom. I found it myself."

Thanks to Grandpa's teachings, there's no place in my house where the tools actually belong. Right now there's a screwdriver in the utensil drawer, a hammer on the rim of the tub, and I just saw a wire cutter on the coffee table. These tools drift from place to place waiting for someone to put them into action on a job they weren't designed for.

My grandfather also taught me how to smoke cigarettes. Not because he wanted me to smoke, but because he wanted me to look natural when he'd hand one to me, which he did whenever my grandmother caught him in the act.

"Here, put it in your mouth," he'd tell me.

"I don't want to."

"Now or she'll kill us both."

She'd come up and grab the cigarette out of my mouth.

"I told him not to smoke," my grandfather would say.

"You're an idiot," she'd come back with.

"I'm not the one smoking, ooh boy."

I realize now that he was trying to joke his way out of it, but I took it seriously when, after my grandmother stormed off, he'd blame me for not looking convincing enough. His advice was to have the Kool Menthol hang from my lip and lower my eyes to look bored, which is advice that I use to this day. Whenever I find myself in a new situation that makes me uncomfortable, a look of boredom comes in handy. Caring looks like you're trying.

He snuck me into Off-Track Betting by putting an old baseball cap on my head and telling people that I was his midget girl cousin. His words, not mine.

"Poor thing. She never grew past the first grade. But she really knows how to pick 'em."

I'd just shrug and try not to talk. We were never in there for long. He'd go to Off-Track Betting the same way an alcoholic goes to a bar—he was just looking for a quick hit.

That could be said about most people at the races. No one is thinking the next race is going to save their life, they're just looking for a little jolt out of the everyday. Win or lose, at least it's something different.

He rarely won, but when he did we'd stop at the Cumberland Farms convenience store on the way home and buy cigarettes and scratch-off games. It was like he wasn't happy winning until he lost it all again and returned to his comforting state of struggle and hardship.

My grandfather sold life insurance and was a good mid-level salesman because he was a good talker. He was funny and warm and wore funny little suits from a time when suits were made from funny little material. His medicine cabinet was filled with men's products that, like his cigarettes, had a menthol scent: aerosol shaving cream, Vitalis hair tonic, high-octane aftershave and the original toxic-looking Listerine mouthwash that didn't even try to look pleasant. These were things that made the nosey child in me worry about what would happen to me when I became an adult.

He did well enough to have a house with a yard, and he even took my grandmother on a cruise once. Cruises weren't as common then as they are today, and this was a really big deal for the family. We had never heard of anyone going on a cruise in our life, so when it was time to go the entire family piled into the car and drove to the pier to see them off.

They even let us come on board, which was terrifying. I was

sure we were going to be trapped on the boat and sent out to sea. Every time they blew the ship's horn, I cried a little harder. This experience was the beginning of my hate affair with boats.

"Tommy, relax, they're just going on a nice cruise," said my mother.

"Someone shut him up," said my father.

But if it wasn't a big deal, why was our entire family there to say goodbye? Now I know it's because they were in awe of the grandeur of it all, but to a kid it was a last goodbye as my grandparents headed out to their watery grave. Nothing calmed me down until my grandfather snuck me a sip of his beer and a cigarette for later.

He mentored a younger salesman, Pat, who followed him everywhere. My grandfather taught him everything about the insurance business and gave him a road map to a better life. He got himself a job and bought a small house around the corner and every day they drove off to call on potential clients in Paterson and Passaic. They were like a comedy team, just two guys from a blue-collar upbringing dipping their toes into the white-collar world. Every Abbott needs a Costello.

I remember my grandfather coming home from work and bursting into the house like he had been chased the whole way. He was overworked, overheated and overwhelmed. His sense of humor was his relief valve, but sometimes it took him a while to remember to twist it open. And apparently by the time I came along he had really mellowed. As a younger man, newly married and raising my mother and her brother, he must have been foaming at the mouth.

There was no talking about your feelings or even thoughts of where the stress was coming from. "Stress" wasn't even a word they used very often, and definitely not as a cause of your rage or insecurity. I saw an old picture of my grandfather recently. He was roughly my age now, but he looked like a much older man. There was no discussion of diet or exercise. You were born and got the body that you got and rode it until it wore out. He ate scrapple and head cheese and pumpernickel bread with herring and pickles.

I think about that anytime a doctor asks about my family health history. Sure, they had high blood pressure; they also ate nothing but fried fat and stopped exercising the day they graduated high school. I'm not saying we come from a great gene pool, but heart conditions should be graded on a curve.

In his later years he did tell me about a meditation practice that he'd heard about on the radio. He hadn't heard the whole thing, but enough to get a handle on it.

"All you do is lie on your back and imagine funnels on the ends of your toes. And whenever your brain starts thinking about shit that annoys you, like work or money or your grandmother, picture the energy going through your body, down your legs, to your toes and out the funnels."

"And then where does it go?"

"I don't know. I guess it flies out the window or falls on the carpet and your grandmother vacuums it up. How should I know—I told you; I didn't hear the whole thing."

We drove around in his little yellow car filled with cigarette smoke and listened to the radio broadcasts of the New York Yankees. He loved baseball, and we would talk about the games and the golden era that he was lucky enough to grow up in, with Mantle and DiMaggio and the rest of the Bronx Bombers.

His humor was irreverent, and he loved to get a rise out of people. He really knew how to make them laugh, which made it really difficult for him when that ability was later taken away:

He had a stroke when I was in high school, and it left him almost mute.

When I got off the elevator at the hospital, not really sure what a "stroke" was, he could see me coming from his room through the glass, and he broke down in tears immediately. His face seemed to flap about helplessly and his big brown eyes were literally screaming out, trying to say everything that the stroke would no longer let him say. I remember thinking that it was worse than death.

It took months of rehab and basic grade-school reading and writing activities to retrain his brain. My grandmother, who so desperately wanted things to go back to normal, actually let him drive. He could barely talk and his motor skills were in and out, but in an attempt to revisit the way they were, she handed him the keys and he took the wheel on a trip to one of our family events in western Jersey. Somehow they made it, and luckily no one was hurt, but the rest of the family intervened and made my grandmother promise not to let him drive again.

My grandmother was crying, not so much over what she had done but over what she had lost, as my grandfather stood there smiling from ear to ear, with a cigarette hanging from his mouth and a look in his eye that said, "I'm back, baby!"

He loved my grandmother with a mix of adoration and need. From the tumultuous early years up until his old age, he relied on the love and caring and patience of his wife.

One afternoon, toward the end, my grandmother went out to the store and left him in the house. He sat alone at the kitchen table in their beloved beach bungalow, which despite his stroke was typically a normal and safe thing to do.

Suddenly he heard a car skidding, and the sound of a crash on the main beach boulevard. He no longer had a sense of time, or he would've been able to figure out that my grandmother had been gone for a while, but he couldn't. He panicked and stood and ran out of the house, terrified that his wife of sixty years had been in an accident. He ran out into the middle of the street and in flailing desperation tripped and fell on the hot pavement.

He was back in the very same hospital where he'd recovered from his stroke. His face was all cut up, a giant Band-Aid on his nose, his arm bandaged. He was shaking and confused. When I walked in, he reached out for me. He was reaching for all of us like a child who wants to be picked up, in the same way he must have been reaching out for my grandmother, for his bride, as he ran out of the house, scared that he was going to lose the only thing he had left. The thing that mattered most in the world to him.

Although he wasn't trying to, he had taught me one of the most meaningful lessons about love that I had ever received—that when all else is lost, love is the one thing that remains. And this was almost as profound as when he showed me how to unclog a toilet with a baseball glove.

THESE ARE THE DAYS THAT MUST HAPPEN TO YOU

I'm not going to tell you how to live because, frankly, I don't know. What I can, and will, and am about to tell you is some of what you will encounter, because despite trying to be your own person and forge your own path, some stuff simply happens to all of us.

There will come a time when you open the refrigerator and discover that one of your roommates has eaten your food. They will do it, they will not admit to it and you will be left frustrated, confused and flabbergasted. Why would someone eat your sesame noodles and then lie about it right to your face? Why would someone knowingly rummage through a shared space and eat what they know isn't theirs? This is scavenger behavior, something vultures and hyenas do. No one wants to share a kitchen with a hyena, so you will eventually move out and get your own fridge. But be careful—there are more vultures at work.

Your car will be towed. Everyone's car is towed at some point. It might be the result of an accident, but more likely it's because of a confusing sign that was put up to confuse you so that they could tow your car and leave you lost and confused.

To call it "towing" is actually too kind. They literally *take* your car, and now you're going to have to figure out how to get it back, and that will be equally troubling and lead you to parts of town that your mother told you to stay away from.

In that same vein, you should learn to fix a flat tire, because you will get a flat at some point, and while there are good people out there willing to help you fix it, there are also bad people who keep a tire iron under their seat so they can kidnap defenseless drivers who don't know what lug nuts are.

People are going to yell at you and make you feel small. Someone is going to call you out at work and in front of your peers tell you about a mistake you made and make you feel stupid and useless. Of course you are neither of these things, and you are doing your best. But even our best is filled with mistakes, and unfortunately there are people smaller than us who like to point out our failings so no one notices theirs.

You are going to fall asleep on the beach on the first day of your vacation and no one is going to wake you and you will suffer the worst sunburn of your life. You will be as red as a throbbing stoplight and it will hurt and because you are embarrassed you will lie to everyone and tell them that it doesn't hurt at all. But it really does.

You're going to throw up in public.

You are going to spend hours getting ready and walk into the party with a tag sticking out of your shirt. No one will tell you about it, because no one ever does, and there's a good chance you'll also have a piece of something stuck in your teeth, toilet paper hanging off your shoe, your fly down and you forgot to put on deodorant.

Some drunk is going to start talking to you in a crowded airport and everyone is going to think that you two are friends.

Someone is going to break up with you. No one has a perfect record, and anyone who says they do is lying or just sensed that they were about to be dumped and acted quickly in order to beat their partner to it. After they break up with you they are going to tell their friends what a bad kisser you are even though you're a really good kisser and everyone knows it, which may be why they broke up with you in the first place.

You are going to hate your friend's boyfriend. Not just kind of hate him but really hate him, and everything about him. And when they break up you will finally have the chance to tell your friend all the things she didn't see, but then they will get back together and you will be forced to fake-laugh and fake-smile till the end of time. Enjoy the wedding.

You are going to wear something stupid but you won't know about it until years later when you see a picture of yourself and realize that there was a time when you had bad taste, no judgment and a high opinion of jean shorts.

You are going to bring a bunch of books on vacation and not read a single line. Don't feel bad about yourself—it happens to the best of us. Sometimes your brain just does its own thing, like a dog who all of a sudden doesn't feel like playing fetch.

Sometimes our brain just wants to bounce from one thing to the other as if it has a brain of its own. My brain is a bully. Every time my body sits down it pokes me and makes me get up again. "Go get some water. Clean your glasses. Open the window. Turn down the heat. Get some more water. Adjust the lamp." It's like an older brother who knows the power he yields and messes with you just because he can. So don't stress—you'll get to reading later. Good on you for at least packing up a few books and giving it a try.

You will become friends with someone no one else likes. You know exactly why no one likes them but for some reason it doesn't bother you at all and in fact it makes you like them even more.

After posting something that you thought was smart or funny or good-natured and cute, people are going to make hateful, terrible comments and make you question yourself, your fellow man and why you even own a smartphone or live on Planet Earth.

You will hear that someone has died and despite what we all know is the right response, you will think, "Good. Enough with that guy already." And you'll catch yourself and want to correct yourself but you won't be able to escape the feeling that the world is a little better now that they aren't around.

You will buy something stupid that is way too expensive and quickly realize that it wasn't worth it and then a short while later do it again.

You are going to throw a party and people are going to either cancel at the last minute or come late and leave early. It has nothing to do with you and your party skills—sometimes no one is in the mood. We're all connected, and sometimes in very silly ways, like for some reason universally not wanting to go out tonight.

You will race and rush during the holidays and wonder why something that is supposed to bring you joy is actually starting to kill you, and no matter how much money you spend or how many invitations you accept you will find yourself late at night standing in the kitchen in your underwear while everyone is sleeping, shoving candy cane cookies into your face because you deserve it.

Life's bigger problems will gather around you like storm clouds and interrupt your plans and make your to-do list seem small and silly. There will be moments when you can't catch your breath, can't find your way, and then suddenly it will all work out.

You will find yourself in a quiet moment, staring at nothing and thinking about nothing. You won't feel sad or happy, or judgmental of yourself or anyone else. You'll just notice that this is you, for the moment at peace, until your mom tries to FaceTime you and blows it all apart.

WHAT GNOMES CAN TEACH US

....

"Below the ferns and mushroom caps, I make a bed and take a nap. I can't sleep too long—there's work to be done gathering pine cones, rosemary shoots and dandelion stalks before the coming rains, and they will come as they always do this time of year. We can't have what happened last year, when I was caught off guard and washed downstream while holding on to an acorn for dear life. If it wasn't for that friendly and resourceful field mouse I never would have survived. No, there is work to be done, but for the moment I need to remove my cap and shut my eyes, because a tired gnome is about as useful as no gnome at all."

This is how I would talk to myself during my childhood while I played in the woods. My mind would rush off to discover and escape into all the magic that I felt around me. Now, as an adult, I actually don't think it was silly at all. There is something out there beyond what we know and I'm still drawn to it, especially as life becomes more and more complicated and removed from the natural world.

I'm a spore, a twisted-up toadstool. I wasn't meant to be plugged into a socket to be recharged. I'm not designed to sit for hours staring at a screen emitting unnatural light disguised as "breaking news." We are nature. We are charged by the sun, moved by the wind and in need of a good pair of sunglasses.

History proves you are a beastly thing, and the natural world is out there waiting for you to return. Even the most disaffected, subway-loving city dwellers can be moved by the inspirational sight of a tree breaking through a crack in the sidewalk, as if to say, "We are both still alive."

A walk through the woods is still an indisputable, unwavering reminder that I belong in the forest, with all its magic, alongside the trolls and the fairies, the warlocks and witches. There is life beneath the green leafy canopy and under the logs. It's busy in the sides of the creeks and under the floating leaves. I've never seen an actual fairy-tale woodland creature, but I've felt them dancing around me in the same way I feel the hum of the trees and rushing of the rivers that create a rhythm for us to bathe in and be a part of.

I was lucky enough as a young child to be able to walk to school. Every morning, with my sisters in tow, I'd head out of the house across the cement garage, out to the asphalt driveway and onto the pavement to my friend Tom's house, where we would knock on his door. Tom was perpetually late, but as he was a year older than me I could push him only so hard. I would start with a hesitant, gentle ring of the doorbell. After no response, I'd give a harder press of the bell, followed by a soft knock. My sisters would start to groan and take a seat on the curb, weighed down by their backpacks and metal lunch boxes. Finally I'd bang with a louder knock and his mother would open the door, apologize and yell for Tom down the hall.

Eventually he would burst out the door and shoot me an angry look as if I were the one who invented school and made him play the trombone that he had to carry back and forth from school every day so he could practice. I can only imagine what his parents were thinking as this angry seventh grader was in his room blowing angry scales against the world.

He would march past us, shoulders slumped, that trombone case banging against his knee, and start the walk down Mulholland's driveway. To call it a driveway is a bit misleading. It was a quarter-mile-long road that wound its way from a street we couldn't see to a giant stone mansion. We entered about halfway up and walked along, a giant cow pasture off to the left, trees to the right, on dark blacktop with rustic cobblestone sides.

Tom would mostly brood in silence while I, used to being around tension caused by tense people—which became the foundation on which I built a career in comedy—would carefully try to win him over in order to create some kind of a fun. I would make jokes, point out something about the day or something I saw on TV or something we'd laughed about some other time.

This seemed a tough task, but all I really had to do was soften Tom up by the time the roadway came to an end between the giant house and the large stone garage. Then, as the pavement turned to dirt, we'd step into the morning shade, pass the rusty and oil-soaked barns and enter the woods.

Whatever mood we were in and whatever complaints Tom had about the injustices of being a kid were no match for the woods. We were no longer students on the way to school, but adventurers out in the wild. The forest calls out for your song and all your creativity and soulful silliness, and we responded by losing our young minds.

We'd scream and run and dance as the trees swayed with applause and the birds followed suit. Tom became one of the funniest people I knew as he turned the trombone case into a battering ram as we marched over the roots and around the bend under the watchful eyes of the hidden raccoons and deer. We'd leave the path and start throwing rocks at imaginary enemies who dared to cross our path.

My sisters turned into wild-eyed spirits, wielding sticks and stomping through mud piles. They shouted profanities at the sky and chewed on honeysuckle flowers, spitting out the stems, the juice staining their sneakers. I once saw my sisters hacking at the trunk of an oak tree with spindly branches in such a rage that I believed they were easily going to chop the fifty-year-old tree to the ground. When we told them it was time to go, they dropped their weapons and looked at Tom and me as if we were next.

The woods are welcoming, but the woods are also frightening. This is where the Big Bad Wolf caught Little Red Riding Hood. This is where the Three Little Pigs had their houses blown in and where witches wait with shiny red apples ready to bake us into pies.

Those stories aren't pulled out of thin air—they are manifestations of our very real instincts that there is trouble out there as well as deep inside of us. They are tales that let the young ones know, and remind the older ones, that the woods and everything in them are to be respected and that if you do you will be rewarded but if don't you most likely will be eaten alive.

Eventually the forest would spit us back out onto the road

that led to the school and remind us of the job at hand. We were no longer free spirits under the watchful eye or woodland gnomes but were back to the school version, the city version of ourselves, albeit with leaves in our hair, mud on our shoes and bark in our teeth. We might be going to school, but we were really creatures from the great beyond.

When I'm alone, standing at the sink, out of sorts and filled with troubles, picking up my phone won't heal me. Scanning through the newspaper won't clear my mind. But a walk outside, for a single, long, temperature-changing breath, most certainly will.

There is a reason my grandmother never missed a sunset. It didn't matter if she was in the middle of cooking dinner or sitting with the family midmeal—when the light began to change and the sun, of which she was keenly aware, was going away, she would announce that it was sunset time and march out of the house. She would march, sometimes with spatula in hand, straight down to the end of the street, or to the edge of the bay, and watch as it went down, amazed every time.

She loved the sun and was in tune with its movements. She would show off her ability to tell the time based on where the sun was in the sky, and she was seldom wrong. Every ending of every day was a wistful goodbye wrapped in a good night filled with hope that she and the sun would be reunited in the morning.

I love a good city. I love a nice sidewalk stroll up to a vintage record store or coffee shop. I like the energy of city life. But that is people energy, frantic and emotional and bouncing off the concrete, and needs to be balanced with earth energy. Unpaved, human-less earth.

Starting in college, my friend Mike and I would pack our

things and head to the backcountry of some national park of our choosing. We started with Yosemite with very little money and even less know-how. I had something that resembled a backpack and he carried a large green army duffel bag. We stopped at a general store and bought two paper bags of groceries and hiked up to the upper lake of Tuolumne.

We looked like we were shopping at a strip mall and couldn't find our car. But away we went, and why not? Why should the lack of proper gear stop us? We had a tent and now we had food, and sure our hiking boots were Converse All Stars and we didn't have a can opener but we were in the woods and that's where we wanted to be and the rest would have to take care of itself.

It took us a full day to achieve what experienced hikers probably did in several hours, but when we got to the top of the trail, which ended in a deep blue glacial lake, any trepidation or exhaustion left us immediately. We set up camp in the most beautiful spot in the world, not another soul around, and it was all ours, until I stumbled on the grave of Bill Stark.

Out in the middle of nowhere, but only several feet from our camp, lay Bill Stark. We didn't know anything about him or how he died or who buried him there. All we could assume was that Bill Stark was there and that he loved the spot as much as we did. The rest of our adventure was in honor of good ol' Bill.

We climbed giant boulders and yelled his name. We called out to him from the edge of waterfalls and through raging winds that turned our tent inside out. We even cursed him, asking him why he didn't tell us to pack a can opener or a hatchet. The fire crackled and the smoke twisted around the three of us, up into the heavens. The gnomes were proud.

Through the years, as our skills improved, Mike and I rode

out a late June snowstorm in the back of the Grand Tetons, stumbled upon a baby moose with her mother in the pine-covered Rockies and danced along the Continental Divide. We hiked through Alaska among giant grizzly bears and ate salmon straight from the cold riverbeds.

And in every one of these places, behind every tree, were the fairies and sprites. The tiny little men with their pointy hats and bushy beards who came out of their burrows to sit, backs against a sturdy root, and share a smoke of sweet tobacco at the end of a long day, sensing from our presence that we were not there to destroy, but rather to visit from time to time.

LONG LIVE THE CLOWNS

....

There are a lot of terrible places in the world. Places that don't have comedy, where people walk around afraid that if they say the wrong thing their lives will be in danger. These are not fun places. They are sad, serious places where it feels like winter all the time, and everyone is precancerous and eats nothing but cold soup with a beet in it.

I don't want to live in these places or allow people to turn this country into one of those places. I don't want to live in Russia. It's cold and scary and you can't find a good cheeseburger. They don't have water parks, they have pools where they drown people for speaking out. Everything is made of concrete and no one wears sunglasses when they drive because they don't have cars and they don't have sun.

They just huddle in their winter coats that they wear all year round on the one bus that runs through town and everyone is missing a tooth and nobody notices because it might cause them to laugh, and no one ever laughs. They just worry about their gout and swollen ankles because they live in a land without comedy clubs, sitcoms or any other comedic way to relieve the pain.

It feels like if we aren't careful, this is where we are headed. What began as a healthy discussion in our culture about the abuses throughout society of marginalized groups has been distorted into a way to destroy artists for their thoughts. These are not well-intentioned individuals, they are hate-filled assassins trying to purge free thought and the expression of ideas, and what is more un-American than that?

Even worse, the fake outrage has given the hateful a place to gin up more hate. By recognizing that the thought police have gone too far and is out of step with rational people, they have hijacked the debate and have found a clever way to go back to the old days of attacking the weak.

There shouldn't be a single article written about the division in America that doesn't mention the lack of television comedies that for decades united us. Look what has become of network television. The networks and advertisers, by kowtowing to the vocal minority of small, pesky letter writers who now have a digital platform, are killing the joy for the much greater majority.

I thank God we grew up in an era of common sense and had the chance to watch *The Mary Tyler Moore Show*, *M*A*S*H*, *Welcome Back, Kotter*, *Cheers*, *Seinfeld*, *The Jeffersons*, *All in the Family*, *Friends*, *Sanford and Son* and decades more of our most cherished comedies. Comedies that reflected who we were, warts and all, and that everyone says couldn't be made today. Can you imagine that? The great American art form, flattened and destroyed by political correctness. That is sick, intolerable and dangerous. At the very least, it's no fun.

Kids today will grow up and be forced to try to conjure up joyful memories and reminisce about *The Bachelor* and *The Real Housewives*. Horrible reality shows putting the worst behavior of people on display without anyone around to make a joke about it. I can see them now, sitting over a bowl of cold borscht, clutching to the holes in their sweaters, in their humorless homes trying to claim that their childhood was fun, that they did and had it all, except for a single, shared laugh.

The insightful and prolific writer Clive James said it best. "Common sense and a sense of humor are the same thing, moving at different speeds. A sense of humor is just common sense, dancing." Well said, and better off lived.

Even if you don't have a sense of humor and you take a joke as gospel, you lack common sense if you target a comedian. Attacking a comedic tweet is giving a pass to the people who are truly trying to do others real harm. Killing the jester is not going to affect the actions of the king.

It's the working people who really need a laugh, and while corporate money may balk at angry letter writers and pull the plug on someone or some project, the regular people, the ones with common sense and their sense of humor intact, are laughing, and are not nearly as alone and isolated as these misbegotten, ladder-climbing creeps.

Comedians understand and express that we are all in this together. It is a crude art form meant for everyday people as we muddle through life. We don't need privileged commentators from the outside telling us how to think by killing our clowns.

To laugh at oneself is to protect oneself and at least make survival more enjoyable. In the middle of the night when I am walking to the bathroom with my creaky knees and wine-filled head, I'll put my arms out to the side like Redd Foxx and waddle through the dark, giggling at myself the whole way. It's not hysterical, but it's funny enough to make me smile and feel better about getting older.

My big-ass Italian family likes nothing more than jokes about other big-ass Italian families. We see ourselves and we laugh at ourselves and that makes us feel good about ourselves. We've been doing this since we got off the boat, and thank God.

Your feelings are hurt? What are you talking about? Is this grade school? Who has time for feelings? What a luxury. I have a prostate the size of a bocce ball, there's a tree about to fall on my house, my dog is throwing up for no reason and my parents won't take their heart meds. Yeah, I got feelings: I feel like shit.

I found termites in my kitchen. We've been to three funerals in the last month, but we can't stop and grieve because we have to keep paying for everything. We have to pay the mortgage and the taxes and the credit card bill, which keeps going up and up and up. No one is asking how we feel about it. My kid needs braces, my wife needs Spanish tile and the cat needs chemo. They're not getting any of it, and I don't feel great about it.

One of the most important lessons you can teach a child is to not be concerned about the opinions of other people. Not only are they useless, but if you allow other people to dictate how you feel about yourself you have allowed them to turn you into a victim.

You can't handle that a comedian made a joke that offends you? There is a list a mile long of stuff I don't like, but it doesn't bother me that it *exists*. I don't like Staten Island, but that doesn't mean it should be removed, it just means I don't have to get on a ferry and go there. Life isn't about how we feel, it's about what we do.

Can you imagine being one of those people who don't try

and laugh about it all, who just take life on its face value and don't try to find the humor in it? That's a terrifying way to exist. It makes for angry and vindictive people, the very same people who are now trying to kill the laughs.

Since my kids have started hanging out with other kids, we've gotten a chance to see how other people live inside those houses around town that we pass by but never go into. Turns out these aren't places we'd *want* to go into. Angry dads, resentful moms, tons of plans and schedules with no laughs. Can you imagine?

I never saw Trump laugh once. He was on a variety comedy game show I hosted and he sat right next to me. Anytime anything funny was said by anyone, including him, he would raise an eyebrow or kind of smirk like a snake but never let out a laugh. That's a house to stay away from.

People who don't laugh go to war with themselves, with their neighbors, with their enemies, because they lack a release valve. They are damaged, sorry, small-minded people, and eventually try to pull down the rest of us.

It's time to start questioning the thoughts of the thought police. Seriously, tell us who you are and why you see a joy-filled art form in this twisted way. We know the person telling the jokes. We know them from a long, deep body of work. They have shown us their personalities throughout the years and we are able to consider the source. Why do you demonize artists; what are you getting out of it? Tell us. Open up and expose yourself and show us everything, as the comedian has done.

Have you been hurt by your loved ones or damaged by your failures? Is that why you have become a scabby, thin-skinned carcass?

What a strange time, that Americans have to walk around

worried about what they say and think. About who they are. I didn't think political correctness was going to be a serious problem when it began. I think it actually helped generate discussion and got us to a better, more thoughtful place. But then I heard people warning us about where this would go and they were right. This ongoing campaign is different. This is McCarthyism from the left and we now sit in a country where books are being banned by both sides.

And that's no joke.

The only way this destructive practice stops is that broadcasters realize there is money to be made in catering to the majority of people who are truly not offended by jokes you could safely tell your priest. Hopefully they are starting to realize that they risk losing money by reacting to a truly small percentage of evil people.

Comedy is love, and love is not something to be analyzed and ripped apart at the seams and dissected by those who don't have it. It is to be enjoyed and shared by the people who get it.

That's just common sense.

YOU'RE GOING TO NEED SOME SPRAY

....

We're overrun with ants. For most of the year they live outside doing their ant thing, happy to eat all the crumbs they find in the yard. But when it rains and their little tunnels spring a leak, they do what every hardworking city dweller does during times of trouble: They pack up and head to the country, where they can relax and recharge.

They descend on my pantry like pushy tourists who think they own the place, and in a way they do. They follow a pheromone trail, a sensory map of sorts that was laid out by their ancestors, which leads to a promised land filled with boxes of crackers, bags of flour and torn-open cornbread mix. They know they'll find bags of potato chips and cereal boxes that were half eaten and never thrown out. And just like generations of ants before them, they'll find a couch filled with popcorn kernels and glorious candy wrappers.

Their entire existence is searching for food, which is a state of mind that I can relate to. "*What's for breakfast? Where's the coffee? Do we have orange juice? Toast? Cereal? Eggs? What about a snack? Where are we getting snacks? Should I look in the pantry? Is there anything in the drawers? What's this on the counter? Who left this pizza crust under the couch?*"

This may sound like ant dialogue, but it's actually my internal dialogue. From the minute I wake up I'm thinking about food. I start by thinking about dinner and work my way back to which coffee I'm going to have with my buttered slice of sourdough toast. Ants may be pests, but they're pests I can relate to.

My wife and daughters see it differently. They're horrified that these dirty little runts are trampling all over us. To hear my wife scream when she sees them, you would think the ants are human-sized and that soon our family will be duct-taped to our kitchen chairs while the ants work us over for our Uber Eats password. Everyone has a limit to what they can tolerate, and my wife draws the line at insects.

In between her trips to the farmers market in search of socially conscious honey and homemade pita chips that she puts in her reusable shopping bags made from recycled hemp-based sweatpants, she is waging an all-out war against bugs.

At least my wife is honest. She's no different from the philanthropist who loves to gamble or the organic chef who enjoys a nice Taco Bell drive-through. She is the nature lover who hates bugs, and in some sort of moral kung fu move she is able to separate her quest to save all of nature while stomping on carpenter ants and leaving their bodies scattered across the kitchen floor like dead soldiers at Gettysburg.

After a certain amount of annoyance even the most sane and compassionate among us turns into a murderer. The war against the insect world has been going on for as long as we've been able to itch—and the bugs started it. Napoleon's army was munched apart by body lice that made homes out of their snappy blue uniforms. George Washington was stricken with a case of mosquito-borne malaria. Even worse, I once had a romantic candlelit bath ruined by a daddy longlegs spider that frightened my partner and sent her running for her car. At least she *said* it was because of the spider.

The itch from a single mosquito bite on a small child can derail an entire family vacation. Skittering roaches, centipedes, moths—the list of undesirables goes on and on, and for all the talk about how we have to save the bees, all it takes is being stung in the ass and having an allergic reaction for you to head to the hardware store in search of some weapons-grade poison, planet be damned.

You're not alone. Take a walk down your supermarket's garden aisle and you'll see what your fellow man has been dealing with. The shelves are stocked to the ceiling with artillery, an array of ant spray, roach spray and wasp spray. Traps, strips and electric zappers. Citronella candles, gallons of poison and spray bottles you attach to your hose to rev up and spray sweet-smelling toxins at bugs that are over fifty yards away from us.

Are we cruel? No. We didn't start this fight. We may have been unprovoked by the whales and the buffalo, but the bugs have been after us for centuries. Sharks kill ten people a year, while mosquitoes over seven hundred thousand. So put your compassion aside and get yourself some spray.

Southern California has a mosquito problem for the first time in its history. When I started coming here in the early 2000s, there was no such thing as closing a window or door, or even putting up screens. After coming from the East Coast, this seemed like paradise. Living in New Jersey means you will be covered in bug spray and welts for six months of the year, but I lived in Los Angeles for ten years before I ever got a single bug bite. Now the place rivals Maine.

Asian tiger mosquitoes who hitched a ride on cargo ships from China have arrived and multiplied and are devouring us all. They are insidious creatures who have evolved to be virtually indestructible. They are black and white, so they can't be seen very easily, and their primary area of attack is below the knee, making it difficult for anyone who doesn't regularly attend yoga classes to swat them.

My wife, the animal lover, has gone as far as purchasing an electrified tennis racket designed to make killing the mosquitoes a sport. She wanders around the house with the racket in her hand like a drunk Serena Williams, swinging wildly through the air. A zapping sound followed by her triumphant scream is our new cry of victory.

I have withstood the threat of earthquakes, wildfires and traffic on the 405, but these tiger mosquitoes may be the thing that forces me to put my house up for sale. There is no end in sight. There are so many restrictions and regulations against the use of poisons in California it's as if they are trying to recruit whatever invasive species is willing to make the trip.

When I was a kid and New Jersey had a gypsy moth infestation that started threatening the health of the trees, that state took a very different approach. It looked around, saw that there were more moths than there used to be and, in true Mafia style, said, "They gotta go."

In those days there were no EPA regulations or committee meetings to get through. There probably wasn't even a form to fill out. All it took was enough people complaining at a barbecue before somebody hired a plane and the city was coated in insecticide like a powdered donut.

This wasn't seen as something dangerous; it was something joyous. Forget protecting the pets and children—someone was finally doing something about the damn moths. We'd run around the streets, faces to the sky, trying to catch the stuff on our tongues like snowflakes. I don't remember anyone suffering side effects, but then again kids didn't complain about feeling shitty because no one listened to us if we did.

After the spraying, the gypsy moths were gone, and so too were a lot of other bugs and probably some species of birds, but people weren't seeking balance back then. They were seeking domination, and if that meant that a bunch of bats, squirrels and other woodland creatures were also killed in the process then so be it. It's not like those other animals weren't a pain in the ass too.

For years there was a very effective pesticide that helped control the legendary New York bedbugs. But when the pesticide was banned, the bedbugs—which were never really gone—must have read about it online, because suddenly they staged a comeback and returned to the city in force. There were reports of entire buildings being infested with them. A friend of mine hammered a nail into the wall, and hundreds instantly spilled out of the hole. People were moving out of their apartments, hiring bedbug-sniffing dogs and trying all-natural sprays that had little to no effect.

The bedbugs ruled the city and the residents had all but surrendered, but then, suddenly they were gone. No more horror stories, no more friends moving to New Jersey and in typical New York fashion no one asked any questions. They were gone, and that's all we needed to know. Could there have been some illegal spraying of a certain banned pesticide? Sure. Is there a chance some hired bedbug hitmen may have been contracted? Who's to say? But one thing was certain: The bedbugs were gone and that was good with us.

But as tough as New Yorkers can be, they are on the losing end in the fight against roaches and rats, which, while not technically insects, are covered in fleas. There's no way to win against these monsters; the best one can hope for is to push them off your perimeter, out of your life and on to the guy next door.

In a strange twist, the insects seem to run from the poison we put out, but our own offspring are clamoring to crawl under the sink and eat all the toxic stuff they can find. Humans might kill insects, but we also spend a lot of time trying to kill ourselves.

From the time they're babies, children chew on soap, stab themselves with the cutlery and stick their tongues in open sockets. It's strange to think that my beautiful teenage daughters walking into the kitchen are the same people I had to stop from drinking Mr. Clean. And if we're lucky enough to get over this urge to hurt ourselves when we're little, we spend the rest of our lives driving in fast cars, smoking cigarettes and having sex with strangers.

I keep a bowl of jelly beans on the desk mainly as a way to attract my family to my office for a visit. During the last ant invasion I walked in and found what looked like thousands of ants crawling all over the candy. It looked like they couldn't believe their luck and decided to lick as many flavors as they could, which is an impressive strategy that I'm surprised I had never thought of myself.

But this is where the ants went wrong. Those were *my* jelly beans, and as much as I admire the ants' work ethic, resiliency and love of food, I ultimately picked up that bowl, filled it with water and drowned the whole lot of them. Then I took the bowl of jelly bean soup full of insect carcasses and dumped the whole thing into the trash. The remaining ants running around my desk like drug addicts who'd lost their friends at Coachella were literally rubbed out by a damp paper towel.

It's us vs. them, and they don't belong in my box of Honey Nut Cheerios, my beloved bag of Cheez-Its or my sacks of bread flour. I have to draw the line somewhere, in the same way that they draw the line around my house and attack as soon as I step outside. It's literally true that it's a bug's world and we're just spraying in it.

THE GOOD AND THE BAD

....

While staring out across a crowded airport, watching the miracle that is my fellow human beings scurrying about, I'll often ask myself, "What's wrong with people?" How could all this potential end up waddling into each other, seeming to care more about their phones and their giant sacks of McDonald's than one another? The answer is simple—bad manners.

The world could be saved if we just had better manners. Those rules of civilized behavior created and practiced by our ancestors can do wonders for surviving the everyday. Simply being polite can calm our thoughtless animal instincts and quickly establish respect between ourselves and the boorish people around us. We don't even have to mean it, we just have to do it. The use of "Please" and "Thank you" isn't just proper, it can literally help us survive by separating the good from the bad.

There's been a dramatic increase in self-centered rudeness throughout our culture. This was on display this morning as a guy on my flight was loudly blurting business-speak into his phone at 6 A.M. while the rest of us were still trying to understand why we weren't still in bed. He deserved a punch in the nose, but that would have been impolite, so instead I just put on my noise-canceling headphones, shut my eyes and pretended I was on my way to Tahiti.

Bad behavior has always been difficult to untangle in this country—Americans have always taken pride in their crudeness and love to put it on display. There is something in our cowboy DNA that loves to spit into the spittoon without caring if we hit the mark. It's a way of sticking out our collective chin and daring someone to say something about it. "In God We Trust" could easily be replaced with "What are you looking at?"

As we devolved into a people that eat fast food with our hands while our bare feet stick out the passenger-side window, I've lost hope that we'll ever get back to the day when people cared about the right way to hold a fork. Who cares whether you should bow or curtsy when you're wearing a thong to your grandmother's birthday party?

Cleaning up our language may be the small, first step we need to take in order to save our civilization. A practiced well-mannered phrase can be almost magical in its ability to get us through everything from business dealings to flirting with the cute bartender who's shaking up our martini behind the bar.

I can't get over how infrequently people use "Excuse me." It's a simple yet powerful phrase that seems to have fallen out of favor or was perhaps never learned at all. Often while sitting in an aisle seat, I will feel a looming presence and look up to find an openmouthed primate staring down at me, frozen in confusion as they try to figure out how to get around me and into their seat. Just say, "Excuse me." Two words that stand ready to serve and that, when spoken, can move mountains—or at least the balding guy pecking away on his laptop.

"Excuse me" is also a nice way to get out of a situation before you do something terrible. When you find yourself in an important business meeting where you're doing your best to impress, a well-executed "Excuse me" is a lot better than standing up, knocking over a glass and yelling, "I really gotta pee."

I hear people saying "Appreciate you" lately. I don't use it, mainly because of its trendiness, but I like the sentiment. People need to feel they're appreciated, so why not come out and say that they are? As my mother would yell when no one was helping her clean up the kitchen after she cooked us all dinner, "A little appreciation would be nice!"

Politeness doesn't necessarily make someone a great person. In fact, the world is full of well-mannered scumbags who use politeness as a devious weapon. There are plenty of smiling, slick-talking bankers in two-thousand-dollar suits just waiting like spiders for you to walk into their webs. The world is filled with dangerous people disguised as courteous social media programmers, advertising executives and cable news hosts. These are the worst of the worst, and while I'm sure there are reasons they turned out this way, it's best to just keep your family away from them and turn off the TV.

On another level there is the everyday bad: the two-bit thieves, pickpockets and friends who don't tip. They are the neighbors who steal your newspaper and the delivery guys who eat your fries and the people who sneak fifteen items into the ten-or-less line. These are not good people, and just because they act out in nonfelonious ways doesn't make their detrimental impact on the world any less toxic.

There seems to be an increase in the number of guys who put

rubber testicles on the back of their pickup truck. Don't do that. I've got a minivan filled with old people and children, and none of us need your truck nuts in our faces. What kind of person does that? A person who never says, "Excuse me."

It may seem like there are more bad people out there than good, but I would argue that they just operate at a much louder volume. Good people tend to go unnoticed if their power is in their gentleness. Truck testicles make a lot more noise than smiles.

There are, however, degrees of good. Not every good deed has equal weight. I tend to talk myself into believing I've achieved a higher state of good than I actually have. I feel pretty proud of myself when I give a good heartfelt goodbye to the flight attendant on my way off the plane. I think, "I bet no one else thanked her like that. Others say it, but I really meant it. Yeah, I'm a pretty great guy." But am I?

I'll give some loose change to someone asking on the street and I'll even donate to a charity here and there, but how much credit should that get me? Shouldn't I follow through one of these days and actually volunteer somewhere, truly helping people?

I think about doing more all the time, especially after a couple glasses of Barolo and a nice aged Gouda. I'll feel so grateful and lucky that the universe tilted these riches toward me that I'll feel I absolutely must return the favor somehow. But it's not enough just to think about all the good things you'll do. The rest of the world doesn't feel the impact of your quiet thoughts unless you really buy into the power of prayer, which based on all the things that I've asked God for and haven't received has left me with a lot of doubt.

I think I'd be a pretty great coach at the Special Olympics. I picture myself providing real guidance and support as I coach the athletes while treating them with the respect that they deserve. I really think I'd be good at it, but thinking it isn't the same as actually making some phone calls and buying myself a whistle.

If I was really so good, wouldn't I be working at the library or helping out at the hospital? Wouldn't I scoop out mashed potatoes for the homeless at Thanksgiving? I think about it every time the holiday rolls around, but then I think how can I possibly help the homeless when I have my own mashed potatoes and string beans to make? Who will watch the turkey while I run to hand out free dinner rolls? Isn't leaving my family on a holiday just being selfish in a different way? And isn't there a saying about how all good deeds start at home? Maybe not, but now there is because I just wrote it, and it's why I don't have to go to the shelter on Thanksgiving.

I will give myself some credit for at least not being a shitty person. I'm a good listener and I ask people about themselves and laugh at their jokes. I do believe that these small gestures are actually quite large, and maybe they're the best I can do. I may not be in the same league as Mother Teresa, but at least I'm not going to ruin your day.

I also don't talk on my phone in a quiet place where no one else is talking or play music from my phone in public without headphones. I hold the door open for people. I say "Pardon me" and "Excuse me" to the point of actually annoying myself. I'm friendly to a fault, which annoys some people, and I know this because when I go by and say hello, only about 60 percent of them respond. The other 40 percent either glare at me or roll their eyes in disgust. But this doesn't deter me, I just keep smiling and waving like an idiot on the freeway to heaven.

Sometimes I give myself a pass because I bring humor to the world and there is a power in that. Truth be told, I would continue to do it even if I didn't get paid. But the fact that now I do get paid kind of takes the charitable edge off the whole endeavor.

Charities seem to realize that there are good people who want to help but who get tripped up by the details. When do you need me? Can I just come once in a while? Are you cool if I cancel because my flight was delayed? They're developing easy-to-use apps that could really come in handy. Pizza Hut has a really good app, and I eat their stuff all the time when I'm on the road just because they made it so easy. So if these nonprofits really want my help, maybe they need to talk to some IT guy or the Pizza Hut delivery guy.

A good way to live is to consider what they will say when you're gone. You want them to say that you were charitable, funny and kind. You never hear a eulogy highlighting how often the dead guy cheated on his wife and cut in line at the airport.

"What a guy! How about the time he stole all that money from his parents and traded in his child's education for that cocaine-fueled trip to Brazil. We're going to miss you, Don."

I love people. I truly do—and although I don't always show it, I want to be considered and remembered as someone who did, even though I sometimes want to kill every dingbat around me.

All in all, I really want this whole thing to go okay. We should all have a good time and enjoy ourselves and have babies and chopped salads and walks on the beach. I want you to have time to read *Confederacy of Dunces* and listen to Coltrane playing with Thelonious Monk. I want you to spend a rainy day drinking a bottle of truly great wine and then collapse on a deep, soft mattress with someone who loves you.

I can't do anything about it, but just know that I am thinking about you. And that's pretty good.

NAVIGATING THE WINE LIST

....

My wife and I were trying our best to have a good time while we sat in a trendy Vegas restaurant on a not very trendy Monday night. The only thing more depressing than Las Vegas on a slow night is seeing Atlantic City when the sun comes up. It's like seeing a magician during rehearsal or Elton John in his underwear.

The main illusion in this particular restaurant was a wine cellar that was a glass-encased tower that stood two stories tall. When you ordered an overpriced wine someone on the waitstaff would be hooked to a metal cable and flown up to retrieve your bottle. Watching a reluctant waitress being hauled up like a fish on a line was hardly worth the two-hundred-dollar upcharge, but like most things in Vegas you just go along with it because "this is what they do here."

The only lesson I learned that night was that while this may be a stupid way to buy wine, it wasn't really any better than the way I normally picked what we drink. My knowledge has improved since then, because I truly love wine. With the right bottle and the right people and the right food, we can be shot straight up to the heavens, where we belong.

Conversely, the wrong bottle can ruin you for days. I recently had the single worst glass of red wine of my adult life. While on vacation, I wandered into an old Italian restaurant in a funky little beach town on the West Coast. Italian places like this are usually a safe harbor, and while the food was comforting enough, the glass of Chianti was criminal.

One sip and my face curled up like a baby trying their first lemon. I waved my arms and stomped my feet. I was in such shock that something could be so majestically awful that I took another sip. It was confirmed. It was an abomination that I obviously can't stop talking about.

I am not anywhere close to being a sommelier, but I do have some basics for you. Anything more specific and you're on your own.

Convenience Store Australian Shiraz—2021

You're in this convenience store because you're in trouble. Someone threw up on something, clogged something or ran out of something. You are stressed (but dealing), and nothing will help this situation more than a ten-dollar bottle of red anything. Screw off the top, screw your problems and screw tomorrow. 2021 is a fine vintage that can be grabbed off the shelf with one hand while you balance the Drano, Tampax Pearls and Wesson Oil in the other. Look for the label with a colorful, cute animal on it that says, "Hey, for ten bucks, what could go wrong?" It's time to forget the damage your adult decisions did to your free-wheeling lifestyle and start pretending that you remember how to party, compliments of your friends Down Under.

Decent Cabernet-Napa Valley—2014ish

This is the bottle that was given to you the last time you had a visitor. It was that moment when they all walked in, handed you an obviously regifted jar of orange marmalade with a checkered-cloth top and this bottle of wine. You glanced at the somewhat familiar label, pretended you knew what it was and said, "Love this . . ." in a voice you'd never used before. Is it the best wine? No, they don't have that kind of money. Is it the worst? No, they wouldn't risk your thinking they don't have money. So you can be confident that, at the very least, it won't suck.

Get out your corkscrew, because tonight you have some other friends coming over and they're the kind of couple who probably pregamed with a couple of White Claws. They aren't looking for a memorable wine, they're looking for just enough alcohol-fueled confidence to be able to regurgitate some of the stuff they heard this week on *The Daily*. Bottoms up!

White Wine—Any kind, any year

This is the stuff from the back of the refrigerator that you keep cold for that one person who can't drink red anymore. Be warned—white wine drinkers cultivate a different kind of buzz. They get a little speedier, a little chattier and they love to bring up an old fight you and your husband had in hopes you'll reenact the whole thing, because that's how they do it on *The Real Housewives*, who are coincidentally also white wine aficionados. The best strategy is to give them a big fat pour, have them finish the bottle in two glasses and hope they turn in on their own and make an early exit.

The Classy Stuff—Probably Pinot Noir—Early 2000s

This is the bottle you got from your business associate during the holidays. You know it's more expensive than what you buy, because your new wine app told you so. You snapped a photo on your phone before the bottle was even unwrapped, and it made you feel like the sender must really like you and so you put it in the closet next to the Triscuits for a special occasion. Well, you got through another day, and isn't that special occasion enough? If you have a decanter you should start decanting, now, even though you're not sure what "decanting" even means. What's more important is to remind your partner how good/expensive this bottle of wine is as you stare them down, making it impossible for them to say they don't like it. You may not like it much either—but this is the most expensive bottle you'll have all year, so fake it if you have to.

Italian Restaurant Brunello—Somewhere in the middle of the menu

Forget learning all the vintages, grapes and terroirs. All you need to do is remember this name: Brunello. If you think you'll forget this, too, put it in the notes on your phone under "Passwords," which is the one spot you will look when you forget what you're looking for when you pick up your phone. There is always enough of this fail-safe wine on the list to allow you to pick one at the bottom of your price range, and more important, when you say it out loud to the waiter you are guaranteed to sound impressive. Try it now. Brunello. Own it. Say it again. *Brunello.* There you go. Forget Barolo: It's too expensive. Forget Montepulciano: You'll never say it right. Forget France, Spain and everyone in it. Just say Brunello, wink at your date and ask about the specials.

Rosé—The one in the pretty bottle

Your brother-in-law who lives somewhere in the 1970s just called you gay. So what? It's summertime 2023 and you've got a crisp, cool glass of rosé in your hand and you don't care who knows it! A hot glass of red makes as much sense as a wool scarf, the white wine is being hoarded by that angry mom over there and your inappropriate brother-in-law is drinking all the beer. So stand tall with your gender-bending glass of rosé, and throw in some ice cubes just for fun. The gals will admire your confidence and the guys will run in the other direction, leaving you to hit on all their girlfriends.

The Half Bottle—Get two!

Your spouse may think you're drinking too much. You may think you're drinking too much. You're probably drinking too much. But this isn't the time to go halfsies! This is the time to celebrate. We've gotten through the Am-I-Going-to-Survive times, past the When-Does-This-End times and have entered the We-Are-Definitely-Going-to-Survive-a-Little-Longer times.

Besides, we aren't really drinking, we are training our sophisticated palates and evolving as people. We're not getting wasted on whiskey and beer. We are just getting by and getting a little fuzzy on wine. But whatever you do, if you find yourself in a quirky Southern California beach town, splurge on a bottle and don't order by the glass.

TO BUY OR LEASE?

....

One of life's big unanswerable questions, along with the very meaning of existence, is whether to buy or lease. Ask your family, your favorite diner waitress or your trusty search engine and they'll all give you different answers and then turn around and defend the opposite viewpoint just as strongly, which means it is yet another one of those questions that proves that no one really knows what they're talking about and you should just do whatever the hell you want.

I suppose at its core, life is temporary and we never truly own anything. Your house, your beloved schnauzer, even that soul mate over there on the couch eating a cookie are all on loan. But while we are here stumbling around in our disposable clothing through our impermanent houses, I will declare that there are some things worth buying.

I bought my first car, a used Toyota Corolla, for twelve hundred dollars cash. At that time there was no question about whether I should buy or lease. I had been thinking about getting my own car since I was a little kid playing with Hot Wheels on the carpet of our basement, so the equation was simple. Get a job, get some money and get a car.

My job was working the breakfast and lunch shift as a busboy at a hotel restaurant named The Orchards. In keeping with the orchard theme, I was forced to dress like a leaf, with an all-green outfit that included a green apron, pants and bow tie, and I spent every day cleaning the discarded food left behind by ravenous businessmen and ill-behaved families. I poured water, fetched dinner rolls and covered for the waiter who was out smoking with his girlfriend in the alley. This was my job, and at sixteen, I figured it was as good a job as I was ever going to get.

By the time my uncle Al, who owned an auto salvage yard, told me that he'd found a working 1976 Toyota, I had enough money to run down to Paterson with a bag bulging with tips. There she was, shining bright in the afternoon sun and in pretty good shape. My uncle had been accurate when he told me over the phone that the color was baby-shit orange, but he had failed to mention the supercool racing stripes down the sides that made the color barely noticeable. My uncle went on about the reasonable mileage and the manual transmission and other mechanical details that I had little interest in. The only thing that I could think about was that this was a real car and I was about to buy it with real money.

When I drove it off the lot, I had the feeling that I had truly earned it. Thanks to all those days cleaning up after others while dressed like a teenage leaf, I had finally earned the right to drive my friends home from football practice. I was now able to drive to the local ice cream shop, where I could flirt with the girl who worked the counter and after ordering way too many sundaes finally muster up the nerve to ask her out. I had earned the sweet freedom that only a prisoner of my parents' penitentiary could understand.

As I drove around town with the windows down and the music playing, my joy was compounded by the fact that this car was mine, something I never would've experienced in a lease deal with no money down.

Sure, I would have had a car that was more reliable and drove me from here to there, but the feeling of achievement would have been replaced by a feeling of borrowing—borrowing from a cold, heartless bank that dictates how hard you drive, how many miles you go and how long you get to keep the car. That doesn't sound like the beginning of a love affair at all.

My relationship with my first car was literally "until death did we part." She was my trusty steed, my partner in crime and my reliable getaway car. She was the chariot who took me to the prom, to football games and house parties. I drove her up and down the East Coast, as far south as Florida and up into the mountains of New England through tree-lined autumns and snow-white winters.

I was a teenager and she was an orphan and I cared for her by providing whatever service was needed in response to whatever needed fixing. When I wanted a new sound system I ripped the dashboard apart and put one in. When a rock hit the windshield, when the brakes started to fail or when a tire blew, she got all the care she needed, and I did it all myself. There were no reminders from the dealership about upcoming service checks or oil changes because there was no dealership. We were like two runaways living off the auto grid.

She was all mine. I decided to put stickers on the back. I decided to rip out the seats and replace them with sexy fake fur-lined replacements. And I decided to install a horn that played over two hundred songs by running a wire directly to the battery, because I had no idea what I was doing but I knew enough to get the system working and annoy everyone within earshot.

She took my girlfriend and me to the movies and on lazy afternoons parked us by the hidden dock in Harriman State Park. We survived close calls like hydroplaning on the way to school in front of an oncoming bus while a carful of young students screamed like we were on a roller coaster.

She drove me to appointments and to the movies and, better yet, to nowhere at all. At a time when the only option for contact with the outside world was to leave your house and go outside, driving held a special place in life. We would drive for hours on end, with no destination in mind. We weren't trying to get somewhere as much as we were getting away from our parents, as we flew by the mile markers, both real and metaphorical, with barely a care.

At night I would park her at the top of the driveway and head inside while she waited for our late-night missions. I would check in before my curfew elapsed, say good night to my parents and wait until the house was asleep and there wasn't a sound. Pulling the blankets off my fully dressed self, I'd quietly open my window and climb out onto the roof of the garage, dangling off the edge of the gutter, my feet finding a railing below where I would secure myself and hop to the ground. Now all I had to do was run around to the driveway, push my car up the small incline into the street and jump in. We would coast, in stealthy silence, lights and engine off, the rubber of her tires mashing on the pavement, as if I were leading a wild horse out of the barn before the break of day.

When we got to the bottom of the street I would fire her

up, hit second gear and take off into the night. We would ride soundlessly through the sleepy, soft cushion of the summer air, to the other side of town, pulling in behind a mass of large bushes outside my girlfriend's house. I'd come to a stop and turned off the engine just as smoothly as we started. The Corolla was just small enough to sit without calling attention to herself, while I climbed through a bedroom window and visited with the other love of my life.

This went on for months without ever running into trouble or getting caught. There was one close call when my Corolla and I ran out of gas on the way home at three in the morning. We were just two miles from home when she sputtered without fuel to the side of the road. I sat behind the wheel in disbelief that I could have been so careless and was about to be found out by my parents or the police. Luckily I found an old hose in her trunk among some oily rags and a can of WD-40.

I snuck up to a car in someone's driveway and syphoned out three or four hoses of gas by sucking the fuel through the end of the tube, carrying it back to my car and releasing it into the tank. It wasn't enough for the owner to notice, but more than enough to save my life. When I guessed that I had enough, I poured some more into the carburetor, and within a few pumps and tries she started up.

We raced back home, praying the entire way. The method upon reentry was to gain enough speed before the final hill so I could cut the engine while still having enough momentum to glide back into the driveway without anyone hearing me coming home a second time. On this night she cut the engine off herself.

After hugging the hood of the car and climbing back into my room, I lay in my bed, fully clothed, covered in joy and gas fumes. Mission accomplished. There was no texting or phone calls; I'd wait until the next day to tell my girlfriend the story. My racing heartbeat started to slow in rhythm with the pings of the Toyota's engine cooling off in the driveway.

Four years later, when my beloved car got older and she was sick and dying, I decided to pick up my five friends and give her one last drive, to the Jersey Shore through the endless, unlit Pine Barrens. It was so dark and her lights had gone out from a failing alternator and electrical system that my friend Dom had to hang out the window shining a flashlight on the white line of the two-lane country highway so that I'd have some idea of where the road ended and trouble began.

We were rumbling forward, pine trees flying by, cold night air thumping in through the open windows, when in the distance we saw a car pull out into our lane, getting ready to pass a giant, slow-moving truck.

We had no headlights. There was no way for them to see us. There was no shoulder to pull off onto. The only chance we had of warning the oncoming car and preventing a head-on collision was for Dom to frantically wave the flashlight into the dark.

The driver barreled toward us. I squeezed the steering wheel, my knuckles shaking. We all screamed a crying farewell scream. At the very last moment we must have come into view, and the other driver swerved, screeched and laid on his horn. We felt alive in that way that only brushing up against death can make you feel. My friends thought that fate had saved us, but I knew it was her.

She was tired and beaten. When we entered town and the police saw us roll through a stop sign without any working lights, they pulled us over immediately. Despite my pleading he made me turn off her engine, and her battery gave out. I had literally run her into the ground, and when a week later her engine seized, I coaxed her back home one last time with the help of the same Uncle Al who had sold her to me.

Battered and rusted and tired and alone, she simply stopped moving. She had given me all she had to give. I gathered my night-sky map from the trunk and my collection of cassette tapes. I grabbed my secret notes from the glove box, my girlfriend's necklace that hung from the rearview mirror. I collected all the items that we had shared and that now only I would need. I was heartbroken as I dismantled the heavy key chain that had been in my pocket throughout my final years of high school. All the keys, yarn bracelets and the plastic Gumby were removed, leaving a single, naked, useless key that I tossed on the seat.

I said goodbye as she was towed away, and at the last minute I ran after the tow truck with tears in my eyes and stopped the driver. With his help, in the hot summer sun, I removed her license plate. That license hangs in my garage to this day as a reminder of what we were and who we became.

That's a love story with a pretty good ending. You don't get that with a lease.

WILL YOU GO OUT WITH ME?

....

Don't abandon it all.

Bring back the school dance. Bring back the prom. Bring back holding hands at fireworks and the summer carnival. Don't let them shame these rituals as if romance is something to be destroyed. There are lessons to be learned from all who came before us about the capturing, nurturing and losing of love. Lessons that feed the spirit.

Don't let them tell you that a double date is corny or that sneaking away from the party together to see a movie or just sit and talk is somehow uncool. Don't let them take away your shared blanket at sunset or your trip with his family to the annual clam chowder festival.

Hang on to these things. All of these rituals. The ritual of spring. The ritual of dating. The ritual of meeting someone, showing interest, asking them on a date, going on that date, hoping for another one, uncovering each other's interests, likes and values all before you ever get that first kiss. It will be a long two weeks, but hang on to these things.

The pursuit of love isn't about instant gratification. This isn't a candy bar to be eaten in two bites, leaving you wondering a minute later if you had even eaten it at all. No, this is a delicious meal cooked by someone's grandmother that needs to be savored. Slow down and realize that this is something special, that it's worth showing the right restraint, the right respect, the right appreciation.

This old path can lead you toward good things. Less confused things. Stable things. There's nothing wrong with a little stability when the seas around us are thrashing about. What some call "old-fashioned," I call "magical."

This is about a visit to the Dairy Queen where we sit in the parking lot under the glow of the fluorescent lights, like kids on summer break. This is about enjoying every minute right up to curfew or talking on the phone and never hanging up. This is about playing within the dating rules that have been set by all who played this game before us because the rules were deemed fair to all sides and gave us—all of us—the greatest chance of winning.

Don't let them tell you that these are outdated traditions from a male-dominated world. To say that men made all the rules is an insult to all the women who came before us. What's more likely, that men came up with rules of courtship or that women were really in control? Who is stronger than a woman? Who is stronger than a mother? Not a disrespectful oaf. Oafs don't get second dates.

Some things in life are better fast. Let them make cars, planes and lines at McDonald's drive-throughs faster. Leave the discovery of the love of your life in a slower gear. Take this ride at a manageable speed, so you can smell the air and see the sights.

This may be your love story—the one story that you tell for the rest of your days. This may be the folktale that will be passed down to the younger generations of how grandma and grandpa met. This shouldn't be a thoughtless one-night stand that you jot down on a cocktail napkin. This story, your story, deserves to be written slowly, in one of those fancy leather-bound books that gets pulled out on holidays and read to the children.

This isn't about speed dating on an app with a tech company as your chaperone. This is a two-way conversation where we look in each other's eyes and see the infinite possibilities of a future together. This isn't about getting some, this is about getting it right.

So strap on a pair of roller skates. Pick a flower. Open a door. Laugh at his jokes. Give her your jacket. Make him a playlist. Invite him to meet your parents. Shake her father's hand firmly while looking him in the eye. Acknowledge to yourself that you can be a part of the family if and only if you win the hearts of everyone.

Say hello to his parents and ask how they've been. Show them that you aren't sneaking in and out on a mission but that you have plans to stay. Make a corny joke and laugh at theirs. This is what spending time together means.

Do these things, these acts that were worked out before we got here, and you will be rewarded. Your embrace will hold within it not just the two of you now, but the future of the two of you.

And if you're really lucky you'll live happily ever after.

FINDING RELIGION

I'm a minister. A man of the cloth. A holy person. It wasn't so much a calling as it was a website. I filled out some stuff online, gave them my credit card and now I am part of the clergy. I did this so I could officiate my friends Noam and Juanita's wedding, which turned out to be a lot of fun, and since then I've conducted six weddings in total and—thankfully—only one confession.

Officiating a wedding is rewarding, enjoyable and enriching. All you have to do is write a little, put on a nice suit and stand in front of a crowd that is already filled with love and hope and funnel that energy back onto the couple. Maintain respect, throw in some humor and you'll be accepting dances and drinks all night.

I'm also a big fan of rituals. They provide a nice storybook for life. For Catholics the story begins when you are born and baptized into the club. When you are around six years old you get dressed up and receive your first Communion. Several years later, you get confirmed and start confessing your sins even if you haven't sinned much, but this practice gives you some ideas that you'll soon get to. Eventually you run into one of the biggest rituals and get married, which leads to a lot more prayers, until finally you are read your last rites, are buried and attend your own funeral. Sort of. That's a life in about five clean chapters.

As of yet I haven't been asked to read anyone their last rites or perform an exorcism, two rituals that I am not qualified for or interested in, mainly because there is very little room for laughs in them. It seems in bad taste to start cracking jokes while the family is clutching rosaries and waiting for you to cast Satan out of their daughter.

Running confession seems fun. I am always very interested in hearing the sins of strangers. Not only do I want the big stories, but I want all the specifics that only a priest gets to hear. Sure it's gossip, but it's the good kind, and the idea of sitting in a booth while people come in and tell you all about their screwups sounds heavenly. I'm sure there's a good amount of small stuff: cursing, using the Lord's name in vain, lying. The next-level stuff would be commonplace infidelity, white-collar crimes and maybe some good old-fashioned thievery. But then we'd get to the good stuff, the holy grail of holy confessions—murder.

I'm not saying every other person coming into the booth would be a murderer, but I bet there would be more than you think. People kill people and get away with it all the time. Most people who murder someone probably wouldn't feel that bad about it and not need to confess, but if you've ever read *Crime and Punishment*—and if you haven't, you should—it turns out that when you kill another human being there's a good amount of guilt involved. Apparently after you club someone over the head with a curtain rod until they stop breathing, it stays on your mind for a while. I know I would have a hard time shaking it off—I feel bad when someone misinterprets a text I sent. I would definitely have to confess.

In the Catholic Church, a priest is forbidden, under any circumstance, to disclose any information that has been confessed to them. So if you're the kind of murderer who really needs to chat but you are worried that your favorite bartender or your brother-in-law the cop can't keep a secret, your only option is to talk to a holy man. That's where I come in.

I always wonder if I've talked with a murderer but wasn't aware of it. I have had my suspicions, especially about my aunt Gladys. She played the part of a dizzy aunt pretty well, but there were many times when I caught her daydreaming with a knife in her hand, as if she knew it had more uses than cutting into a block of Wisconsin cheddar.

I'm not sure exactly how I would handle a murderous confessor. I'd have to be hard on him, make him say some prayers and stuff so he understands that all his killing is wrong, but on the other hand I wouldn't want him to be so angry that he turns around and kills me too. It's kind of like when your friend comes to you for support after he's cheated on his girlfriend. You want to let him know that what he did was wrong but at the same time not turn him off or else he won't tell you any more cool stories about cheating on his girlfriend.

The closest I got to hearing confessions was at a wedding, but, like most things in life, the fun expectation bumped up against the real thing. I had just completed my fourth wedding and I was making the rounds at the cocktail reception collecting my praise when an older gentleman sought me out. He seemed to be reeling, hurting and longing for relief. He was such a mess that he clearly didn't consider that I might not be a real priest, and if he did, he didn't care. He walked up, saw me with a martini in my hand speaking with some friends and blurted out, "Father, may I have a word with you?"

That felt pretty cool. I've never been called "Father" before, and I have children.

"What is it, my child?"

"I have done something very wrong. Very wrong indeed. And I need to confess."

Anyone who's been to a wedding knows this is definitely going to be the most interesting conversation of the night. Most of the evening will be spent talking to strange family members you've never met before who have nothing more interesting to talk about than how bad the traffic was. I took one more sip of my martini, passed it off to my friend and guided this lost sheep to the couch.

"Have a seat, my son."

We sat somewhat out of the scrum but where people could still hear us. I leaned in so he didn't have to shout, which he didn't mind doing. "I've cheated on my wife."

Someone laughed.

"Oh, well, that's very common."

"No, you don't understand. I've cheated on my wife *a lot*. Like over a hundred times."

"Well, I'm sure you've been married a long time."

"Two years. She's my third wife. And the strangest thing is that I never cheated on the other two. Not once, and the marriages went to hell. But with Barbara I can't stop cheating, and I'm telling ya it's the happiest marriage I've ever been in!"

Wow. This guy was bold. He was misguided. He was starting to make sense.

"Does she—does Barbara . . . know about your infidelities?"

"Of course not. If she did, the whole thing would be over."

"I see."

"Yes, you see? This is the pickle I'm in. I know I shouldn't cheat but if I stop, my marriage will be over. You've got to help me."

A server came by with a tray of lobster sliders. I took two.

"Well, I'm sure 'a hundred times' is an exaggeration."

"No, it's not. I keep track. I have it in my phone."

"Well, that doesn't sound like a good idea."

"No," he said, "it's okay, because it's all in code." He took out his phone, and sure enough he had an elaborate system in his contacts with the names of every one of his secret partners broken down under three different companies. This way if his wife ever checked on his phone she would likely scan past his business contacts having no idea that they were actual naked guardian angels responsible for her marital bliss.

I didn't focus on the number or the names, but from the speed of his scrolling I assumed that around a hundred was pretty accurate.

"Why so many?" I asked.

"Because I don't want to fall in love with any of them. So I have to keep moving."

"And you really think that if you stop it will hurt your marriage?"

"Oh, I'm sure of it. I tried once, stopped for like two weeks. Without even thinking about it I started packing my suitcase. No, I can't stop. Out of respect for my wife."

Another server came by with champagne. I took two. I was out of my league. I needed to start with small confessions like lying or using the Lord's name in vain, but here I was face-to-face with quite possibly one of the greatest adulterers of all time. I was confused. I was lost. I wanted to hear more.

"So what do you want me to do?" I asked.

"I want you to do what you do. You know, forgive me."

"You don't even know me."

"Yeah, but that's what you people do."

"What do you mean, 'you people'?"

"You people. You Holy Father types. I need you to forgive me so I have a clean slate."

"And then you'll stop?"

"No, I'll keep going, but I'll be starting fresh."

He basically wanted me to hose off his dirty car. He knew it would get dirty again, but that didn't mean it wasn't worth at least cleaning it up for the next day or so. This was hard logic to disagree with. Aren't we all just wandering around gathering up dirt? Isn't cleansing what forgiveness is all about? This cheating son of a gun was downright poetic. I was impressed.

I'm not a real holy man. I haven't studied the Bible or the Koran or read Stephen Hawking, but I do have a sense of right and wrong. And although I have no real power and wanted him to know that, I looked him in the eye and said, "I forgive you, my child."

He welled up with tears. "Wow. Thank you, Father. I feel great." He grabbed me in a bear hug. He was very handsy.

"What do you feel so great about?" asked an attractive woman in a sleek red dress.

"Honey, I'd like you to meet Father Tom. Father, this is Barbara, my wife."

I almost passed out.

"I hope he wasn't talking your ear off, Father."

"Oh, he doesn't mind, it's all part of the job. Hey, Father, why don't you give us your number for when we renew our vows."

I haven't done a wedding since.

WHY WE MARRY

Let me explain why you are better off married, and not compared to torturous death by tweezers but compared to most things. Life is an endless cascade of choices and decisions and mental buggery. Any way that we can cut back on the sheer volume of problems and what-ifs makes us better off. That's why marriage is the ultimate fix. Saying "I do" is a great way to say "I don't" to a whole bunch of problems.

No longer will you be walking around thinking about asking someone out. Wondering if you said the wrong thing or if he'll like your shirt. You are in for the long haul, and life's little trivialities that could trip up a less solid couple are now brushed off like a weak little gnat.

You no longer even have to worry if your partner likes you very much. Liking you is beside the point. You can rest assured that there will be many times when she won't like you, and that's okay. You're not in this to be liked all the time, you're in this because she doesn't totally hate you.

Dating is a nonstop worry. It's a constant check on your self-esteem and repeated kicks to the nuts of your ego, leaving you vulnerable, nervous—a wreck! Some people enjoy this kind of thing and like being tested at every turn. These are the same masochists who can't stop getting tattoos because of how it feels or sign up for things like boot camp and go on three-day fasts.

When I see married couples, I see people who are relaxed. People who understand the joy of a nice pound cake. People who aren't so distracted with finding someone new that they have the time to appreciate the subtlety of a nice hand-roasted coffee. You don't discover that kind of thing when you don't know whose bed you'll be sleeping in next.

When I was single, trying to couple up was constantly on the top of my to-do list. I'd run around flirting with cashiers, hitting on girls in bars and showing up at parties dressed like someone I thought other people would want to go home with. I'm not great alone, which I'm told isn't so healthy, but it always seemed much nicer to climb under the covers with someone warm than sit by my lonesome on a psychiatrist's couch.

Being alone is simply not as much as fun as hanging out with another person. All my favorite activities, like cooking and drinking good wine and hiking through the woods, are much better shared. I like to talk with people and explore who they are and all their ideas. I was pretty much done exploring all of mine by the seventh grade. Some therapy-loving single person is most likely dissecting these words and coming up with some unresolved issues that I have been carrying around since childhood, but not everything has to be fixed, especially if by ignoring it you get to share breakfast with someone else.

For someone who makes his living talking in front of large crowds I should be more of a narcissist (another trendy psych term), but I like spending time with other people, especially women who like me right back. Now, if you make the wrong connection you'll be back to feeling just as isolated as when you were single. But find the right one and suddenly you belong to something bigger, and after marriage it gets even bigger, because then you add a whole bunch of other people to the mix.

In-laws, cousins, crazy aunts and uncles and of course the ones who fill up your household under the titles of children and pets. This is all much messier than the life of a bachelor who comes into his lifeless apartment, tosses his keys in the tray by the door and does whatever he wants, whenever he wants, till the end of time. But that's not a life for me.

Don't get me wrong—there are times when I'm so tired of being around all the people in my house that I find myself standing alone in a dark utility closet like I'm playing hide-and-seek by myself. It helps to restart things, because no one is looking for me and after a day or two of isolation I'll wander back into the kitchen, ready to talk.

I like being married because there isn't an option of leaving. Of course you can always separate and divorce, and I don't recommend this course of action, but—like certain medical procedures—you may have no choice. However, once you're in a marriage for the long haul and you sign, as I did, a "no-divorce clause," you are in it for good. We also have a "no F*You clause," because there is a real hurtful power to that word that should never be used against the person you can never leave. F-bombs are called "bombs" for a reason.

If you get in a fight while you're dating, you can leave at any moment, because you have that option, and that's a horrible option to have. If you do leave, you have to gather up your laptop and all your chargers and go back out into the world and start lying to people all over again about how great you are.

Married couples aren't leaving during a fight, because they don't have that option. My wife and I could get into a horrible argument and I know I'm not leaving. No, when we fight I go to the pantry. I go to the pantry and I eat a sleeve of Girl Scout cookies while I stare at my reflection in the toaster oven. I do this until I feel so disgusting that I forgive her for whatever it is she said to me because I know she's probably right because she's married to a monster person who just ate twenty-four Samoas while standing up.

I don't have to even worry about looking good or staying in amazing shape or wearing cool single-guy clothes. I get clothes when she's getting clothes. That's how married couples end up looking alike.

She'll say, "I'll be right back, I'm going out to get some sneakers."

"W-w-wait a minute. I need sneakers too."

"You do? Do you want to come?"

"Yeah, I want to come. Let's go! It's Sneaker Day."

And we head off to Foot Locker and we sit in the married section and they bring out sneakers that haven't been made for any athletic event whatsoever. They're big and they're white and they have Velcro. And they're good for standing, while we wait for each other.

"Should we get some socks too?"

"You read my mind! Socks, shorts and sneakers. Don't bag them up—we're going to wear them out."

Do we look good? No, we don't look good, that's not the point. The point is to make each other unfuckable to the rest of the world. We don't need some pervert looking at our cool shoes and making a move on us. That would ruin the whole good thing we've got going.

It's important to marry for the right reasons. I have a friend who's considering marriage, and he's thinking about all the wrong things. He keeps wondering if the girl he's with is "hot" enough. So dumb. As if being hot has anything to do with marriage. You don't marry hot, you marry strong. You want someone who can pick up the other end of the couch. Without taking the cigarette out of their mouth.

Marriage is a contract to join forces and make life more enjoyable by making things easier. And if done right you gain a whole new set of freedoms that you never had before. The freedom to wear a sweater with holes in it for a week straight. The freedom to watch birds playing in a birdbath for an hour or two rather than scroll through dating apps to see if you have a bite.

It's not always easy. There have been plenty of times when I've walked into the kitchen and caught a look of disgust, just a quick glance that tells me I'm in trouble. I know her so well that I understand the meaning of every facial tic, every flick of an upper lip; they let me know, "Uh-oh. Today, she hates me."

And this is when I know that I'm in deep trouble and must react the way that the Scouts tell us to respond to a grizzly bear in the wild. Centuries of DNA that is programmed deep inside us tell us to run, but we can't. Bears are much faster than us. She may not look it, sitting over a bowl of wheat bran in her quilted winter robe, but this is not someone to mess with.

There's no fighting this bear. The best case scenario is that you'll get in a punch or two before she rips your face off. Not an eye, not a patch of hair, but your entire face, like a rubber Halloween mask.

The Scouts remind us not to make eye contact. You have to make yourself big and stupid and indecipherable so as to confuse the beast. Make loud noises that will hopefully repel them, but if they do charge, lie on the ground and play dead. Of course, you can only do this for so long, and if the bear is really angry the one thing you will have to do that is not a part of the Scout handbook is to have sex with that bear. That's right. Mount it, stroke it, take it to dinner . . . whatever your technique is—you make love to that bear, pray for forgiveness and hold on to your face.

The best approach is to lower your expectations. I don't say that as a way of demeaning marriage—quite the opposite. I think that's why people break up: They have too high an expectation of what they are going to get out of this one relationship. It's best to be realistic and not overanalyze.

My grandmother always told the story of how she met my grandfather. They met in a park; he loved her right away and she couldn't stand anything about him. She didn't like how he looked, what he was wearing or what he had to say.

"I thought he was the worst, but he just kept coming around, day after day after day. He just wore me down and eventually I thought, "What the hell, I guess I'll get married."

They ended up married for over sixty years. Was it heaven on earth? Was it nonstop romance? Not even close. But they never expected it to be, and that's why they lived happily enough ever after.

HOW ARE YOU FEELING?

....

How are you feeling? Pretty good? Not so hot? Did you start off feeling good and then slipped momentarily into great and then crashed and felt like garbage? Do you feel okay except for that long list of stuff that's wrong with your body and won't go away? Well, welcome to the never-ending, ever-expanding life as a living organism. You're just as itchy and blotchy as the next gal, so stop worrying about it and get on with your life.

Jump on the internet, and before you finish typing out what ails you Google will complete your sentence because you're not the first one to ask. I just typed in "What's the white thing . . ." and Google filled in: "on my lip, on my tongue, in the back of my throat, on my eye, in the corner of my eye, on my nail, on my tonsil and on my nipple."

It's nice to know I'm not some kind of monster, but it is a somewhat disgusting reminder that there's always something wrong with us. Right now I'm feeling pretty good, but I know it's just a matter of time before I discover a mystery scab on my bald spot or feel something weird on my eyelid that the internet will confirm is ancient mystery fungus.

Of course, the main objective is to stay alive, which is why whenever I hear that someone has died the first question I ask is, "How?" I may seem like I'm concerned about the deceased, but what I'm really thinking is, "How do I make sure I don't die like that?"

I can protect myself from most of the bizarre accidents I hear about simply by adding certain activities to the list of things I'll never do. I can guarantee you that I will not water-ski into a pier or miss the target while skydiving or be eaten by an alligator in the Amazon, because none of these things happen in my living room.

I won't be stuck in the ice on Mount Everest, because I'm not going to Mount Everest. I won't even watch a documentary about climbing that dumb mountain, because anytime I watch any documentary I am brainwashed into believing every word of it and I don't need anyone planting the idea in my head that climbing that thing is a possibility.

I won't be trapped in a cave or stuck in a well, and I won't be killed while trying to surf a hundred-foot wave. I'm not going to die in a bullfight in Spain or while playing Russian roulette in an underground prison camp or be trampled to death in a moose-hunting accident in Siberia. I don't even know if there are any moose in Siberia, but I'm not even going to look it up, because I'm not going.

That doesn't mean I'm safe. I could easily inhale some printer toner or explode from eating too much bread or drinking too much Barolo. I take my life in my own hands every time I light the grill with an extra-long match or use that really hard loofah my wife keeps in the shower.

But while we can all try our best to learn from each other and avoid death, there are smaller, non-life-threatening conditions that we just have to deal with. These are unavoidable regardless of how well guarded our lives may be, but the good news is that they can be managed with stuff readily available behind the counter at any local gas station.

You can take comfort in the fact that you're not the first person to have an ingrown toenail or a creepy case of pink eye. People have been dealing with plantar fasciitis since they were running away from Genghis Khan. There were women on the Mayflower who were not only seasick but bloated and irritable. I guarantee you that someone at the Last Supper simply couldn't eat one more piece of g#ddamn bread.

A walk down any aisle in CVS will confirm that whatever problem you've got has been dealt with by millions of scratching and complaining brothers and sisters before you.

Have a splinter of wood stuck in your hand? Here are some tweezers. Have something in your eye? Here are some drops. We have rubber things that suck the water out of your ears and droppers that shoot stuff into your eyeballs.

There are ointments and salves and sprays. Supplements, antacids and antibacterial sponges. We've got stuff for your gas, your aches and your snoring, and they're all time-released and fast-acting.

We can help you stop smoking, start sleeping and get rid of your headache fast. If you've got a cough, cold or flu, need braces and supports and a whole list of stuff for your allergies and asthma, we've got a brightly colored box with a coupon attached.

This doesn't mean that when you are faced with an ailment it won't feel like you're the first one in the history of mankind to be this miserable. I was thirteen years old when I came down with the worst case of poison ivy ever recorded. I had a brutal mass of blisters behind my knee that popped and spread every time I took a step or bent my leg. It got to the point that it looked and felt like I was carrying a roll of Bubble Wrap behind my knee.

It itched in a way that I'd never experienced before or since, and although I knew the worst thing to do with poison ivy or a mosquito bite or anything itchy is to scratch it, I couldn't deny myself one of the best feelings in the world.

Have you ever had a mosquito bite and rubbed sand on it? Have you ever run hot shower water on an itch in the middle of your back? Have you ever had poison ivy when you were thirteen, grabbed a toy rake and attacked it? I have. And it was the dumbest, most glorious thing I have ever done.

I went after my poison ivy like a dog going after a flea bite covered in barbecue sauce—wild-eyed, panting, tongue out, sweating, oblivious to everyone who was yelling at me to stop. I dug in, felt the relief and entered a deep emotional state that I couldn't get out of until my owner, in this case my father, smacked me on the backside with a newspaper. I knew I had done wrong, and had never felt so good.

My mother brought me to the doctor to see if there was anything to be done about my growing mass. More than her concern for me was her worry that I would embarrass our entire family on our upcoming vacation. It would be hard to avert the stares of horrified strangers while sitting poolside with old Bubble Legs.

No one likes going to the doctor, least of all a thirteen-year-old boy in the full throes of puberty. The last person you want to see while you're trying to hide the weird changes that are happening to your body is the pediatrician who's been treating you your entire life. Not only has he seen every change, ailment and embarrassing thing you've ever gone through, but he's kept records.

"So, how's the bed-wetting?"

"I don't do that anymore."

"That's great. Mom, I bet you're pretty happy about that."

"I would be if it was true."

"Okay, get off the table and take off your pants."

There's nothing like standing in your underwear in front of your mom while the doctor takes a look under the hood.

"Hey, look at that, you've got pubic hair."

At this point I'm praying that his next move is to stab me with a scalpel and put me out of my misery.

"Okay, so I hear you've got poison ivy. Let's have a look and see what's . . . Good god! What have you done? You know you're not supposed to scratch it, right?"

After more humiliation and scolding, this medical professional with all the answers sent us away with cortisone cream and some calamine lotion, two things that do squat. I spent the entire vacation in the hotel room caked in pink cream while my family swam at the beach, built sandcastles and ran around on their blister-free legs. There was nothing else for me to do but stay in a dark room and wait it out while listening to the moody early techno sounds of Yaz on my Walkman.

Puberty is filled with unsolved mysteries. The toughest case to crack was acne. I was a regular old pizza face. We tried everything, and I say "we" because I recruited my entire family in the fight. It was a horrible thing to go through, and I was desperate.

Here I was, doing my best to make friends and be attractive to girls. I was working on jokes and developing charm and thoughtfulness and then I woke up, looked in the mirror and saw a face filled with zits. It was as if they spelled out "Go Away" to anyone who looked in my direction.

I tried pads and ointments and special soaps. I had doctor visits where they would shoot needles into my face. It was like having poison ivy on my head. Nothing worked until they came out with a brand-new experimental drug called Accutane. It's still around, thanks to the young pioneers like myself who were the pustule-covered guinea pigs in the name of science.

It was a really powerful drug that sucked all the moisture out of my body, leaving my face with fewer pimples and my lips without skin and my throat without saliva. It turned my entire body into a desert and made it really tough to make out with my girlfriend. After every kiss I had to drink some water and coat my molting lips in ChapStick. Very sexy.

Another side effect was a spike in my cholesterol level. I was a healthy young athlete with the cholesterol numbers of a middle-aged man living on a buttered hot dog diet.

The only thing that truly worked, which is the case for most of these ailments, was time. I wish my doctor had been honest and told me that we just had to let nature run its course all over my body and eventually, while my pride might be damaged, I'd be okay and better prepared for whatever the next humiliating phase would be.

The ultimate ailment is age. As we get older we all try to fight the years the same way I was trying to ward off pimples, but there's no Accutane for that condition. Wobbly necks, eyes that don't work, hair falling out of your head, weird spots, moles and growths are all unavoidable, and while we buy up all the miracle cures, the best we can do is to accept the fact that we can't turn back time.

If you're over fifty and a little chubby, I don't care how expensive your workout outfit is, there's a good chance that when you're cruising down the street you look like a Peanut M&M. But hey, at least you're getting your steps in, and that's got to make you feel pretty good.

A CHRISTMAS TOWN HERO

....

When Christmas comes under attack, I stand firmly in my slippers, sharpened peppermint bark in hand, ready to fight back. And I'm not talking about the drummed-up phony attacks stoked by the politically manipulative, heavily makeup-caked faces of cable news. I'm talking about real attacks like the one I was forced to fend off this year when I was called upon to save Christmas from attacking robots.

I wasn't looking for this fight, but heroes seldom are. I imagine that I felt as ill equipped and ill prepared as those who came before me, namely Rudolph the Red-Nosed Reindeer, Frosty the Snowman and Tim Allen That Guy From *Home Improvement*. They didn't ask for this fight either, but when called upon you rely on whatever strengths you have, and mine is my undying love of Christmas.

I love it all. I love the food, the lights and the travel. I love the tree, the presents and the decorations that fill the house. I don't care if it's sappy or commercial, life is short and if you give me a reason to play more music and eat more treats, I'm grabbing a spot on the couch, sipping some Lagavulin and drifting off to the North Pole.

I will admit that my love of Christmas has very little to do with my own free will and everything to do with my mother. My mother is and always has been a big promoter of Christmas. She's been Santa's hype man since the good old days, filling us with cookies, candy canes and tales of what would be waiting for us on December 25th. Parents have a powerful ability to mold the minds of their children, and she injected us with so much folklore that we had no choice but to lose our little minds and join the Christmas cult. This is the same way that unsuspecting children end up Irish step-dancing and attending monster truck rallies.

My guidebook on how to save Christmas came from the training films I watched during my childhood, in the form of Christmas specials. There were only a handful of them, made all the more special because there was nothing else for children on television other than a run of Saturday morning cartoons. We got one part of one day to be entertained by TV, and if you missed it you wouldn't have another chance until the next week.

Thankfully, we didn't miss many Saturday mornings, because we didn't grow up in the era of nonstop sports and activities that ate up every hour of every weekend. Back then a seven-year-old's baseball career wasn't a real high priority in the community or the family. Things like time off for the parents and time to be a kid were seen as more important than watching uncoordinated children try to hit a baseball.

I recommend you keep your kids out of as many organized activities as possible. I know they tell you how important it is for your child to be on the traveling team because they could be the next Derek Jeter or prima ballerina, but if they are telling you that and asking for money at the same time, keep some perspective and give yourself and the family some free time.

So, when a Christmas special, made for children, appeared on a Tuesday night, it was nothing short of a Christmas miracle. We'd talk about it for weeks ahead of time, from the moment *TV Guide* told us it was going to be on. Yes, that's correct—all the information about what we could watch came in the form of a weirdly shaped weekly magazine or in the back of another dirty relic, the newspaper.

Christmas specials were mostly crude stop-motion animation, but to our little brains that were still amused by things like spin tops and View-Masters, they were nothing short of magical. I don't mean to claim that life in the 1970s and '80s was as puritanical as *Little House on the Prairie*, but compared to today it was pretty close.

It was obviously a much simpler time, and out of a simple time came simple pleasures, like celebrating the holidays in a way that was almost religious but more fun, because we actually didn't pay much attention to the religious part.

Once Frosty and the Grinch started to appear on TV, the next big event was going up into the attic to get the Christmas boxes out of storage. My father would pull out the ladder and push me up there, because why have a son if you're not going to make him do things for you like crawl on his belly through a cobweb-filled attic. I had no choice, because as much as the attic was clearly filled with ghosts and demons, it was also where Christmas was stored.

Once I was up there, he'd hand me the family flashlight, with its perpetually fading batteries. Keeping an extra set of fresh batteries might be something that other people did, but not us. We weren't those kinds of people.

"Do you see the boxes?"

"I can't see anything. The flashlight's broken."

"Shake it!"

"I am."

"No, really shake it. Like a man."

After pounding on it for several minutes like I was giving it CPR, I was able to somewhat see. Not from the faint glimmer that came from the dying bulb, but because I was up there long enough that my eyes adjusted to the darkness like a cat's.

I'd grab the crumbling cardboard boxes and pull them back across the exposed beams to the attic opening, where my father was waiting. He would hand them down to my mother, who would assess the inventory. And of course every year there was always one missing box.

I'd poke my head out the opening.

"I want to come down."

"She says there's one more."

"There's not. Please, I want to get out of here."

"Just look around! She says there's another one."

My mother yells, "Who's 'she,' the cat's mother?"

"I'm telling you I don't see any more."

"Give the flashlight another shake."

Having retrieved the box or not, I'd eventually be allowed back among the living, then try to make out the decorations I hadn't seen since last year as my eyes adjusted to the light. My sisters and I would rifle through the boxes, frequently holding up a snowman made out of Styrofoam balls, a fat Santa door knocker crafted out of a sock or some other long-lost treasure.

"Ooh, remember this?" someone would yell.

"Ooh, I remember that!" the rest of us would respond.

This went on for a while, as one by one the house would be filled with decorations from over the years. It created the same nostalgic effect that I now experience from the first martini of the night.

Today, I have to retrieve my boxes from a utility room off the garage, where the same fears of the dark come back to haunt me. I have to turn the light switch on before the door closes or whatever lives in there will have its chance to get me. I try to laugh it off. What grown man is afraid of the dark? Judging from the way I frantically reach for the switch, that man would be me.

As we get older, the holidays force us to reflect. They are yearly markers in our lives that demand some accounting of where we are and who we've become. This year I found myself decorating the house alone. My children are getting older, and they no longer come running with excitement when I pull a stuffed Rudolph out of the box. There's still some enjoyment there, but not the screaming, running and dancing of earlier years. Even Rudolph, with his fading fur and weakening song, seems to be trying to tell me those days are gone.

But that's okay. This is yet another phase in a lifelong celebration. I've unpacked Christmas boxes in different places, surrounded by various family members, since I was a child, and it's second only to the fun of setting up the train set and Christmas Town.

My first train set as a young boy went in a small circle around the tree. We had a tiny plastic village that was connected by a single wire, which caused the homes to pull in on each other and fall off balance. But when the room was dimmed and my first Christmas Town came to light, I was hooked.

From that point on, every year the residents of Christmas Town have enjoyed an expansion. It began with a snowy blanket and better homes. A proper train was added, and each year more and more tracks. The town's population continues to grow, with new villagers moving in each year. There's the preacher who stands outside the church and the mom pushing her stroller through the windy streets. There are the skaters and the kids building the snowman and a businessman twice the size of everybody else, who sits on the bench outside the pizza shop.

And the city has grown to accommodate the population boom. There is a grocery store, an apartment building and some new homes. There's even a trailer park with a nearby tattoo parlor and the politically incorrectly named Hobo Town, where the residents celebrate the holidays around a garbage fire but seem warm and happy.

Christmas Town has really been the most special and carefully planned-out place in our entire house. It captures the imagination of everyone who visits, and it's a wonderful thing to see kids of all ages getting down on the rug to work the train and take in the sites.

But this year trouble came to Christmas Town.

Everything seemed to be going along as planned. The grocery store was lit up and a man perpetually walking his dog stood out front. The kids were building their snowman while a herd of reindeer looked on. The homes were lit up, with plastic trees standing at their sides. Snow covered the ground and the train was parked by the gazebo on this peaceful holiday evening. It seemed as if nothing could ever go wrong.

But then a slightly ominous rumbling sound was heard approaching in the distance. It didn't seem like a threat at first. It was far away enough that whatever it was, the people of Christmas Town needn't worry—the problem was in some far-off place.

The rumbling grew louder. The tiny people on the bench started to shake. Santa seemed to point from the rooftop. And there it was—the Roomba, the robotic vacuum, making its rounds. It seemed innocent enough, and everyone seemed relieved that it wasn't something more dangerous. The obedient and always mindful Roomba buzzed by Christmas Town, and all was well until it turned back.

Now the Roomba seemed to be moving with intent. It sounded different. It sounded angry, and it was heading straight for Christmas Town.

Should I have raced toward it and turned it off? Sure. But when you're two Scotches in, curled up on a comfy chair by the fire, sometimes you don't act as quickly as one should. And I trusted the Roomba. I had seen it dodge dog dishes and go around table legs. I'd marveled at its ability to change direction when it sensed a staircase or power cords. It would surely turn back when it hit the train tracks.

But it did not. In an AI rage, as if it was out to devour Christmas itself, the Roomba jumped the tracks and gunned it for Main Street. The people had no time to react. Actually, they had no *way* to react. They just stared in their frozen poses, hoping that someone—that I—would jump in and save them.

But by the time I heard the whirling, sucking sound, the damage had already been done. I jumped up and grabbed the Roomba as fast as I could, but I was too late. The feet of the little boy who'd been making the angel were sticking out of the vacuum hole. The snow cover was torn and sat bunched up against the pizza parlor, which now lay on its side. It was a bloodbath.

There's no hospital in Christmas Town. Bodies were lined up on the tracks. The preacher said nothing. And worst of all, Santa was gone. Christmas Town had been razed, our leader was missing and Christmas itself was doomed.

Quietly, and somewhat drunkenly, I went through the town like FEMA after a hurricane. I disconnected the Roomba and put it in the recycling bin. I was in shock as I looked at the overturned pizza parlor. I tried to reorient myself, now without the town Christmas tree to go by. It's all a little fuzzy, but I think I remember the preacher choking back tears.

But as people often do after a tragedy, I swore that we would rebuild, and slowly Christmas Town started to come back together. Sure it was damaged, but its spirit was intact. The people of Christmas Town are resilient and strong.

Even with a skid mark across his face, the young boy returned to the snowman, in a sign that the townspeople might be down but they'd be back. The snow was torn up, but now it had history.

Yet, as optimistic as I was, I couldn't help but think that we were all lying to ourselves. How could Christmas survive without Santa? He was the heartbeat of our town, of Christmas itself, and now he was gone.

And then out of the darkness, up in the limbs of the tree above, I saw something that the plastic people from Christmas Town could not, because their necks don't move. I saw, underneath an icicle ornament, a little foot in a black boot. I reached up and tugged it out. It was a Christmas Miracle. It was half of a Santa.

I restored his legs with his partial torso back to the rooftop. Sure, he didn't have that beard or hat or head, but anyone who knew Santa from the waist down knew it was him. The mom didn't look up and smile from her stroller, but I knew she wanted to. I started up the train, took a sip of Scotch and watched as Christmas Town rejoiced. Were they calling out my name and thanking me? In their own way I'm sure they were, but I don't like to talk about it.

That's not what The Man Who Saved Christmas would do.

NEVER TRUST CHILDREN WHO DRESS AS ADULTS

There's a disturbing painting in our guest room, which is really my wife's office, sometimes a sewing room and the all-the-time dog room. The painting, in a yellow frame, hangs above the bed, and depicts one of the things that I'm most scared of in life—a small colonial boy dressed like an adult.

He's about five years old and has short blond hair that's combed to the side like a sinister soft serve ice cream. He's dressed in a blue suit with a puffed-up tie, like a miniature Thomas Jefferson walking the grounds of Monticello at springtime. His pants go down to the knees and he has long white stockings and little leather hooflike shoes. He is standing with one foot up on a step and his small elbow resting on the railing as if he's posing for the cover of a corporate annual report.

His clothes may say that he is a mannerly young lad, but I'm not fooled. His beady little demonic eyes say that not only is he going to get you while you sleep but that he's done it to others before you. And he has a condescending smirk that says, "I know that you think you're onto me, but we both know that you'll never catch me." And as if there were any more evidence needed that he's up to no good, his other hand is deep in his little vest pocket. Why? What does he have in there? A knife? A letter opener, a vial? I'm afraid that by the time we find out, it will be too late.

I'm not saying that all children who are dressed like adults are murderous criminals—just the ones who *like* being dressed that way. It's not normal. All children at one time or another end up being forced to wear something their parents made them try on, but a normal child will ditch the belts, bow ties and bowler hats as fast as possible. If a child enjoys being dressed in hard, vinyl, high-heeled shoes and calmly walks around sipping on a martini and looking with disdain at the other children, he is a psychopath.

This isn't a kid in a fun outfit, it's an advanced adult mind dressed in a disguise. This is a highly skilled, satanic killer playing the role of a Goody Two-shoes. He knows that in order to get away with a murder it's useful to look like the unlikeliest of suspects. That way, when the dead uncle is discovered in the apple cellar with an ice pick through his eye, everyone will blame the loud, sloppy kid. No one would ever think that Kevin in his corduroy suit could have done it.

I think these little phonies are to blame for a lot of the world's unsolved crimes, great and small. Think of the petty crimes, the unexplained things that happen around the house. The missing car keys, the limping cat, the broken vase. These odd occurrences that are blamed on forgetfulness, failings and phantoms are more likely the work of devious young ne'er-dowells. While the other children are playing hide-and-seek, they are playing hide dad's wallet. While their sister is playing house, they are gathering matches to burn theirs down.

I'm not in law enforcement or enrolled in detective school, but I would guess they don't spend a lot of time training new recruits on how to catch child criminals. I have, however, watched a lot of unsolved mystery shows, and not once does someone suggest questioning the kid wearing a blazer and carrying a briefcase. They're trying to solve the mysterious house fire, missing jewels or cars with failing brakes by collecting DNA? It would save them a lot of time if they started looking for tiny footprints.

This doesn't guarantee that you'll catch these insidious and clever little shits, because a small colonial boy won't kill someone in an obvious, sloppy way like bludgeoning them with a mallet. That's beneath him. The child that is cunning enough to dress in a velvet vest with a pocket watch will kill you by arranging accidents that can't be traced back to him. Loosening the screws on the underside of a stool. Slowly exposing the end of an electrical wire. Feeding the dog an ancient herb that slowly makes him go insane before he eats his owner.

Those little pockets are a great place to hide poison. Poison is small and sneaky, just like children. We can all understand murders of passion: A husband walks in and finds his wife canoodling with the butcher and cracks the butcher's head open with a lamp. It's much more troubling when you hear about a local prized pig that was slowly poisoned, found its way into the butcher shop and sickened and killed the butcher at the counter. That's another level of evil that could only come from a tiny person's pocket.

When I was a child, I dabbled in crime. But you have to

realize, dear reader, that it wasn't me choosing this path, it was the gum. I was in fourth grade when Bubble Yum was invented. Before then the best bubble gum you could find was as hard and flavorless as a plastic fork. If you were lucky, you would get two or three chews of flavor before all traces of bubble gum left your mouth, leaving you with nothing but a flavorless, grueling workout for your jaw.

And then Bubble Yum shows up. Six gigantic individually wrapped cubes of pure, soft bubble gum. The second a piece was unwrapped you were engulfed in a haze of candy goodness that you knew was going to last. It was soft, tasty and able to do something all other bubble gums failed to do—blow amazing bubbles.

It was so glorious that kids were unwrapping Bazooka gum, throwing it to the ground and stomping on it with the heels of their sneakers. They were opening up packs of baseball cards and feeding the free gum inside to their dogs. We didn't have to suffer the humiliation of trying to act grateful when we all knew our childhoods were being shortchanged. We now had Bubble Yum, and we were in bubble heaven.

The only problem was that this miracle of a gum cost fifty cents a pack. That was forty-seven cents more expensive than Bazooka. That was fifty cents more than any of us had. The gum was out there, but it was beyond our reach. We didn't have jobs. We didn't have money. We barely had pockets.

If we were going to get some Bubble Yum—and we were absolutely going to get some—we would have to steal it. There was no question of whether this was right or wrong. There was no discussion about what would happen if we got caught. Like I said, we weren't at the wheel of this getaway car. This was a crime of passion.

We didn't even have a plan. We just knew where it was and we got on our bikes and we pedaled our gangster butts down to the store. We were so badass we didn't even use kickstands, we just tossed our bikes on the ground and walked inside. If there were kids from another school there we would have rumbled. If there was an old lady in our way we would have knocked her right on her ass.

The manager had to have been onto us the whole time. Three penniless kids shifting around, probably wearing bathing suits, no parents, no wallets, no good. It's strange that it wasn't locked behind the register in bulletproof glass. It was like the early days, when the authorities had no idea that over-the-counter cold remedies could be transformed into hard-core drugs.

There it was. In all its enticing glory. The packs had a shine to them that spoke of the magic inside. This was new. This was unlike anything any other generation had enjoyed. This was made to blow not only bubbles but the minds of school-aged children around the country, and it was working. We had something good. Something new. Something ours.

We were bumbling bank robbers who thought only as far as getting into the bank. We were in a haze. We weren't thinking straight.

Our strategy began and ended with "Get the gum." We figured that all we had to do was muster up enough courage to grab it and the rest would take care of itself.

We acted as if we were the only ones in the store, egging each other on out loud, announcing to everyone what we were about to do.

"We each take a pack."

"Why just one? Who made you boss?"

"Okay, two. We'll each take two."

Shoppers began peeking down the aisle at the chaos as we got ready by stretching, running in circles and clapping our hands like we were psyching ourselves up for a weight-lifting competition.

"Okay, everybody ready?"

"Ready!"

"One, two . . ."

"We've got this!"

"Yeah, baby!"

"Three!"

"Get it—go, go!" we screamed, and grabbed all the gum we could. We stuffed some into our bathing suits and under our chins and dropped more on the floor. I opened a pack, unwrapped a piece and shoved it in my mouth as if my mission was completed and the heist was already over.

The manager, who had been waiting for this moment, came barreling down the aisle.

"Hey you kids! Get over here!"

He came stomping after us.

"Run!" I yelled with pink saliva drooling down my chin.

We scattered like crime-riddled cockroaches, spinning around in circles, climbing the shelves, laughing and screaming at the same time.

I, fueled by an acute feeling of Bubble Yum–induced invincibility, decided to run full speed ahead straight at the manager. I thought that he wouldn't dare try to stop me and that if he did I would run over him like a freight train. I took off.

"Where are you going?" my friend yelled.

Through pink spit, I let out what I thought was a lion's roar but what must have sounded like a kitten's sigh and ran right into the leg of the manager. He didn't struggle. He wasn't intimidated. He simply squeezed my shoulder and it was over. Eyes spinning in my head, focusing on nothing, like a dog caught with his head in the trash, I was caught. I came in as an innocent boy looking for gum and was leaving a convicted shoplifter.

While sitting in the back office waiting for my mom to come, I had time to reflect. I wasn't cut out for this life. I knew that stealing was wrong without my parents having to say it. I wasn't a criminal, I was just a kid dressed like a boy who should have been swimming with his friends. And that's why I got caught.

If I had been dressed in a three-piece suit I could have quietly walked in, slipped the whole box of Bubble Yum in my briefcase and walked out with the admiration of everyone in the shop. I would have returned back home, where I would have sat in my room, proudly blowing bubbles while I waited for the poison to kick in and kill my grandma.

But that wasn't me.

What purpose does a little person have in being dressed like that if not to infiltrate the adult world and start doing adult things? And these will not be good things. A six-year-old doesn't put on hard dress shoes and a tie in order to relax with older people. He puts on this uniform to mingle and drop arsenic into some unsuspecting woman's drink. Or to wander off to the dining room in order to slip a silver-coated steak knife into his pocket.

This is where bad people come from. In the same way that not all old people are cute and cuddly, not all children are good. Some are evil, and they know their way around a bow tie.

SLEEPING TOGETHER

....

The goal of flirting and dating is to eventually end up sleeping together. And if all goes well and you fall in love and marry and live together, you will share a bed for the rest of your life and you will be miserable to the end of your days.

It doesn't start off that way. Sharing a bed when you're young is heaven. You're attractive, healthy and strong. You can have sex all night long, end up passed out in each other's arms like a pretzel twist and sleep in peace through the night. You wake up so rested and happy that you have sex all over again.

There is no morning sex where I live. There is rage and anger and finger-pointing about who ruined whose sleep last night.

"It was you. You should have heard yourself," I'll say.

"Oh, no. It was you. You need a doctor. There is something seriously wrong with you."

The truth is, it's probably both of us. Because we're over forty, and if you are over forty you have a 50 percent chance of getting a good night's sleep on any night. Because you're dying. You're slowly dying, and your body is trying to choke you out and technology is keeping you alive.

I'm right there with you. You have a 50 percent chance of sleeping well tonight, and not because you did something crazy. Not because you went on a cocaine bender, no. Someone had a cookie after 6 P.M.

"Oh no. Donna had cheese at the party! She's not going to breathe right for a week."

"Bob had three beers! Welcome to the fart palace."

Growing old together sounds like a cute achievement of a happy marriage. Holding hands as you walk down the street, helping each other through life. Delightful. But when you're both falling apart, sleep is not something you enjoy, but something to be endured, and one person's issues are the other's insomnia.

My wife has a lot going on.

She grinds her teeth in her sleep. She's so stressed, or anxious, or angry that she is grinding her teeth down to nubs. And rather than figure out the cause of that—which to be frank, I don't want to dig too deep into because chances are that source is probably me—they instead give her an NFL-issued mouthpiece and put that in her mouth like a chew toy from Petco.

She gnaws through three or four a month like an angry beaver. I wake up with bits of plastic all over my face; and they're big and blue and glow in the dark. That's how I know if we are going to fool around at night. If I see a blue floaty thing coming across the room, I know that it's not happening. Not tonight, because she just put on her equipment. She puts on her headgear and her mouthpiece and her eucalyptus ointments and climbs into bed with her unshaved legs like a koala bear. An angry koala trying out for the Packers.

She gets up to pee more than I do. She's like a middle-aged man in a Flomax commercial. I didn't know that women could have an aging prostate, but she does. She gets up six or seven times a night, and when she walks her ankle pops. It's loud. I can't hear it during the day over all the leaf blowers and garbage trucks, but in the quiet of the night it's the loudest sound you'll ever hear.

When the popping mixes in with trying to breathe around the mouthpiece, it sounds like Darth Vader is trapped in Bubble Wrap in my bedroom.

I'm sure I'm no angel. I've been told—though the evidence is far from conclusive—that I snore on occasion. From my cheese addiction I can only imagine that once in a while I might let out an adorable purr that may or may not be heard by the person whom I sleep with.

To be honest, I am getting to the unfortunate age when whatever I eat or drink during the day will have an effect on how I sleep. It really sucks. I love eating and drinking just about anything. Never in my life have I had to think twice about having a cup of coffee after 3 P.M. The only reason to not eat something spicy was whether or not I could stand the heat on my tongue, and not that it would make my stomach grumble at four in the morning and cause me to have nightmares and terrors and writhe around on the mattress in a wrestling match with myself.

I remember when my mother realized that she could no longer eat garlic. If she had even a bite she would be up for days. This sounded absurd and impossible to me. Not eating garlic? You might as well spit on your Italian ancestors' graves. I remember thinking, "Who cares if it hurts—you power through. It's your duty to eat garlic."

I maintained this arrogance until the night a dish of pesto

kept me up until daybreak. Part of it was the stomach pains and part of it was fear that I too had succumbed to this weakened state brought on by age. Any new developments as one ages are not improvements. Your eyesight doesn't get better. Your hearing doesn't improve. You don't become more flexible and remember what stories you've already told. No. When you start to fail, you fail for good.

We're a lot like an old car. At a certain point, after some minor repairs, the problems just become too many. The leaks and dents and misfires become too much. Eventually the mechanic, in this case your doctor, just looks at you and says, "At this point it just doesn't pay to try and fix her."

But I will rail against this. I will fight this fight. I will not go quietly into this bed. I will eat garlic and cheese and drink too much wine. I will live like I did when I was twenty, even though I'm snoring next to my lover like a fat man in a Mafia movie. When I sleep on my back I snore so loudly that I wake myself up, but when I sleep on my side my stomach makes noises and when I sleep on my stomach I wake up with a stiff neck and sore shoulders and need about twenty minutes to regain the feeling in my fingertips.

They should just put me in a stall like a horse. Cover my eyes. Put a blanket over me and let me stand there until it's time for my morning oats. Which is pretty much the only thing they give me for breakfast anymore.

I love my wife and I've tried everything to convince her we should sleep apart. I tell her that I still love her but we should sleep in separate rooms.

I tell her, "Someone is leaving tonight. Someone is getting their pillow, kicking the other one and leaving in a rage. So why not do that at ten, with a nice peck on the cheek?"

I tell her that "I'll go. I'll sleep in the guest room. I'll sleep in the garage. I don't care. I'll do anything. I just don't want to sleep with you."

And that's when I lose her.

HOW TO RELAX

DAY 1

We're starting our annual vacation in an idyllic beach house on a street lined with pastel homes and plastic-coated lounge chairs. There are signs the shape of lighthouses and beach umbrellas with the family name etched on them and an American flag flying outside every house and it feels like they are flown for all the good reasons.

I know a vacation in such a place should be a wonderful and peaceful idea, but it is one that fills me with a good amount of dread.

It's not the place or the beach or the signs. It's the relentless expectation of having to unwind and enjoy myself before the vacation ends. It's a race toward relaxation that is mentally exhausting.

I am wound pretty tight. I wouldn't say I'm outwardly nervous or anxious, but like all of us I have a lot of responsibility and carry the weight of that wherever I go. In order to unwind I have to truly forget about all of it and focus on the smaller concerns like getting drunk at 10 A.M. in flips-flops and a T-shirt with a dolphin on it. It's like a vacation meditation of sorts—a yoga practice in order to become mindless.

When people go on vacation, they say they are "going to get away for a while." You get away from things that can do you harm or even kill you. You have to get away from trouble. You have to get away from monsters. You grab your keys and frantically run to the car, pray that it starts and take off down the street. And a couple times a year you have to get away from your life before it devours you.

But this is getting harder and harder to do, because we are never disconnected from our lives anymore. Before technology took control of our lives, all we had to do was leave town and not tell anyone where we were going. You could actually disappear and no one could find you.

There was absolutely no chance that if you heard a phone ringing while you were sitting at an oyster bar in Puerto Vallarta it would be for you. Only in extreme cases or dire emergencies would someone perform the herculean task of tracking you down, but by the time the manager had pulled the phone with the long wire across the restaurant up to your booth you'd know something was wrong. You'd take a drag of your cigarette and tell the dame next to you to keep it down while you took the call and learned who died.

Today, we live on bad news, and it finds us everywhere we go. I'm so used to being hit with bad news that the only real fear I have is learning that my phone has died.

DAY 2

On the second day I woke up with the same feeling that I have when I'm home. The feeling of a looming deadline, or an appointment I have to get to. It's that nagging feeling that I get when I wake up at home and the first thought is "What do I have to do today?" The answer while on vacation is "Nothing," but the fact that I'm waking up with that feeling shows I haven't reached a vacation state of mind, as was evidenced by the number of emails and voicemails I scrolled through.

When I was a child my parents would take us down to the Jersey Shore, to a house where there was no phone or television. While the technology existed, my father refused to install it, in order to ensure that when we went away we were really away, or as he put it, "So no one can fuck with us."

If we wanted to make a phone call we had to walk to the Laundromat on the boulevard where there was a single phone booth. We had to grab fistfuls of change, actual coins, and dump them into the phone in hopes of making a three-minute call.

My father was once away on a trip and planned to call and check in with us. This had to be planned a week in advance before he left. On Wednesday at 6 P.M. my mother and two sisters and I put on our raincoats, walked through a storm and crammed into the phone booth. We pulled shut the door and waited for his call. He never called, and after some time we gave up and walked back to the house, where we resumed playing Trivial Pursuit by candlelight like the shipwrecked family we were. We weren't worried, we'd just missed the call, or he hadn't placed the call, and this kind of thing happened all the time.

There was no way for the news of the world to find us, either. We had a radio, but no one was suggesting we gather around the kitchen table and tune in the AM station in the hopes of news from the front. We didn't even have a mailbox. If someone back home wanted to tell us about the chicken pox outbreak or a pipe that burst in our home, they couldn't do it.

And we didn't mind. Looking back, I'm not even sure what stressful life we were trying to get away from. What was tormenting us back then? The newspaper that landed at the end of the driveway? That one half hour of news a night on Channel 7? Those pesky three phone calls a week? Today that sounds like the peaceful vacation state of mind I'm currently trying to achieve.

The perverse effect of having all the news all the time is that we think that it's our responsibility to digest it all. As if it is now our job to be informed on every aspect of every story. Am I going to do something about it? Am I going to act once I learn about the injustices in Syria or Hong Kong or the Sudan? Or am I just going to walk around feeling worse about the world, the times and my pounding headache?

We've attached devices to ourselves that turn us into shit receptors. We have become live flesh-and-bone antennae receiving nonstop messaging. For what? Why? We just receive and process and sit. The messages we receive don't make us get up and do something. They don't thrust us into action. They make us click more and more until we go to bed, where we are so stressed that we stare at the ceiling for six hours.

We have our caveman instincts to always be on the lookout for danger, and now we are receiving high alerts all day long. Every time we look at our phones our caveman DNA reacts like someone is yelling "Dinosaur!" into our cave. But the dinosaur never comes. We just poke our nervous system until we become unfeeling, unfazed and unable to enjoy our lives or our vacations.

During the pandemic and the election and the insurrection, it felt like we had to watch the news every moment just in case we had to pack a bag, grab some bottled water and head out of town. But even then, where were we supposed to go? It's not like a dictator takes over our democracy and we all just meet in the desert and draw up plans in the dirt like a game of pickup touch football.

And to be honest, the one thing I hate more than violence in our capital is being stuck in traffic, and I can only imagine what the roads would be like during the early hours of the apocalypse. I'd prefer to let the unraveling go on for a while before I start up the car. Traffic will be a lot lighter when the streetlights stop working and the zombies have eaten a bunch of us.

As I said, I'm technically on vacation, and these are the thoughts that are still bouncing around in my brain, which is pretty good evidence that I'm nowhere close to nirvana.

DAY 3

My instinct to shut everything out in order to have a good time or at least clear my mind was correct. And I haven't achieved it just yet, and I'm starting to feel guilty about it.

I swore that I wasn't going to use my phone at all on this trip. I've been pretty good, but that's not something you say when you've gone cold turkey. "Pretty good" is how you describe looking at the phone briefly in the morning, once at lunch, as soon as you get back from the beach and for a good half hour right before bed. Oh, and another twenty minutes or so when you can't fall asleep and think reading will help, but you can't see your book in that light even with your glasses so you open your phone and cram some information about the mistakes we made in ending the war in Afghanistan. But I promise to do better.

I am writing on a laptop, but it isn't connected to the internet and I haven't asked for the Wi-Fi code, which means that technically this computer is as distracting as a typewriter, which isn't distracting at all. I'm in pretty good shape except for my phone that's sitting next to me on the table which it has to be right now because my friend Robin said she might stop by and it would be rude to not respond to her while we are both in the same vacation spot at the same time.

The social aspect is really the part that keeps me checking on things, but that's the entire problem with these miracle devices, isn't it? You pick it up to do that one virtuous activity, like connect with a friend or look up a recipe for focaccia, and you immediately get sucked into a host of other more insidious acts that we are trying to avoid on vacation, like checking emails, *The New York Times*, Slate, Instagram and Twitter.

But the social part also extends to the people I'm here with. My daughter was complaining that her mother, my wife, never responds and that they rely on me to keep in communication during the day about the important logistical items like when are we going to the beach, when are we coming back from the beach and is it okay if they go shopping instead of the beach.

DAY 4

Today was a good day. I'm starting to feel vacationy, because I've finally admitted that I may need some outside assistance, and I smoked pot in the bathroom. Suddenly my phone wasn't an issue—I didn't even remember where I put it. I had much bigger issues on my mind. Snacks.

The way it works down here is you load up your bag with some essentials and walk about a half mile to the beach. It's not a long walk, but it's just far enough that you aren't running back to the house to fulfill every need. My schedule is to head down around ten in the morning after morning coffee and stay till around one, when I come back for lunch. After a refueling and reapplying sunblock, I return to the beach from around 2 to 5 P.M.

I'm not one to load up a cooler and drag that to the beach. I'm going to the beach; I'm not moving in there. Some people have lost their minds and think that because they waddled their asses up to the ocean it's their right to build giant tentlike structures that look like something out of a Roman military encampment. They have coolers filled with shit and pee in the ocean. They have to. They are drinking cases of beer, and because they have blocked out the sun they don't have to go back to the house and take a break. There are no public bathrooms, so they are peeing in the ocean.

This may sound gross to you but honestly, after a lifetime at the Jersey Shore, it's the least of our worries. The oceans have come back to life nicely in recent years, but for decades that wasn't the case. For a while there was a lot of illegal dumping going on. We in New Jersey blamed it on the New York Mafia. It might have been the Jersey Mafia, but we all knew it was the Mafia.

We would find medical IV bags, used syringes and plastic garbage. It really was awful. The Jersey Shore beyond what was seen on MTV has some of the nicest beaches in the world. This is not an exaggeration, and to have it littered with garbage was a sin.

One summer an actual toilet washed up on shore. A white porcelain toilet. But as is the way of people from New Jersey, they weren't as much horrified as amused, and pulled it up onto the beach and starting sitting on it and taking pictures.

But those days are gone, and the protection of our oceans has translated into real practices, resulting in an ocean teeming with wildlife and the occasional family from Bayonne that pees in the water.

But not me. I pack light, go lightly and now that I was high all I needed was the right amount of snacks. I needed Chex, Cheez-Its and a bottle of water. This sounds simple, but when you're high it's as complicated as packing for a weeklong camping trip.

But with the focus on the mundane, the big life stuff started to blur into the background. Problems with world events were replaced by problems with my flip-flops. Urgent calls from my agent were no longer as important as attacks by seagulls.

And of course getting a little high was just the kick start into the vacationland that I needed. Not enough to be too high, but enough of a reality adjustment. There's a reason Jamaica runs on weed.

DAY 5

A revelation!

I'm happy to report that I'm pretty chill. The feeling of being relaxed on vacation that I was faking in the beginning has now genuinely taken hold.

Not only was putting the phone away a very important and utterly necessary thing to do, but there was an even bigger realization: All the overworked people who had come and opened up their beach umbrellas decades before me had already worked out all this vacation stuff. All I have to do is follow their lead and do the dumb vacation things that you're supposed to do.

Go get some taffy. Get on a goddamn bicycle and pedal your fat ass to a candy shop and buy some taffy, fudge and while you're at it some Swedish Fish. You don't do this at home. There aren't a lot of candy shops set up at home by the bank and the funeral home, but there's a bunch of them on vacation, and there's a real good chance they'll be right next to the ice cream shop.

Do that every night, too. I don't care if you have dairy concerns at home. I don't care if your lactose problem causes you to light up the night sky with your own fireworks display. That's your other life. This is vacation. And while you're at it, keep some extra cash in your beach bag, because the ice cream man is coming to the beach and he's going to ring his bell and you (or a child you can bribe) are going to run up and buy a Chipwich or an Italian ice right in the middle of the day.

Spend the day in your bathing suit. I hope you don't do that at home. You shouldn't. There comes an age when wearing a bathing suit as pants is no longer allowed. Of course, there are exceptions, based on where you live and what you do for a living, but short of being a surf instructor in Malibu you should be wearing some real pants. But not on vacation.

It's actually required that you wear your bathing suit—into the ocean, back onto your sandy chair, back home, in the car, at the store and off to dinner that night. This subtle gesture will change you. As the expression goes, "Dress for the job you want," and in this case that is no job at all.

Eat, drink and be merry. In addition to candy and ice cream, there is a whole list of things that you need to eat and drink to send your soul into vacation mode. Clams, donuts and my favorite, crumb buns. Crumb buns are also known as coffee cake, but in New Jersey they're so much more. They take a coffee cake and put giant crumbs on top, coated in confectioners' sugar. It's more sugar than you have eaten all year. And this is breakfast.

Lunchtime? How about a margarita? Or maybe a beer? Day drinking, sweating, napping on the beach.

Just follow the rules. It's all been worked out for you.

DAY 7

I can't believe it's time to go home. Just when I've really and truly relaxed we have to pack up our stuff and hit the road before next week's renters come in and take our house. One week wasn't enough—we should've rented for two. We do this every time. But at least I'm relaxed. I think I'm relaxed. I hope I'm relaxed, because leaving this time of a day means that traffic is going to SUCK!

TRY NOT TO LIE

....

I had a college friend who loved smoking pot with his parents. At that age we weren't fans of anybody's parents, but in this case we made an exception. We could get off campus, drive to Ed's house, spend the night and smoke all the weed we wanted right in the kitchen like we were drinking milk. The price we had to pay was listening to his nonstop, unbelievable and inexhaustible lies.

His family lived in a rural part of western New Jersey that looked like it belonged in Oklahoma. It may be hard to believe when landing at Newark Airport that you're anywhere near open fields filled with cows, but drive out Route 78 long enough and there are all sorts of livestock, hillbillies and anti-abortion billboards. They were so far out into the country that even though Ed grew up in Jersey, he spoke with a southern drawl.

His mother would open the door with her long spindly arms

and peek her head through the opening like an expectant spider. She had long gray hair that she kept out of her eyes with a homemade beaded hippie headband. She was taller than all of us and would bend down to kiss us hello while holding our faces in her nicotine-stained fingers.

If this had played out like an eighties teen movie, one of us would have ended up in a bubble bath with her, but the only one she seemed to be attracted to was her son Eddie. They were close. A little too close.

But we didn't care. We were getting high and making giant Italian dinners that, for college kids who felt like we were close to starving most of the time, were heaven-sent. We chopped up tons of garlic, poured in cans of fresh tomatoes, basil, tomato paste, salt, pepper and oregano and boiled three pounds of pasta, all while smoking our faces off and listening to Ed's tall tales.

Being around Ed was exhausting. He never stopped talking. He was like a ventriloquist dummy that was talking all on his own. And when someone does that much talking, they are eventually going to run out of the truth. Eventually they've got to start making stuff up, which he was more than happy to do.

He told endless stories about the heroic and dangerous things he did when he was on vacation, at home or anywhere there wasn't a witness. He fought off gangs of three or four hoodlums with his kung fu kicks. As a teenager he once robbed a bank just for fun. A husband walked in on him having sex with his wife, and without stopping Ed turned around and said, "You're gonna have to give me a minute, I'm not done yet." The husband was so scared of Ed that he just shook his head and went back downstairs.

He was made of 100 percent, grade A, American bullshit.

Look, everybody lies. Everybody at some point is going to change a story to fit their needs. And those needs might be as big as staying out of jail or as small as not feeling stupid for spending so much money on running shoes, but we all do some colorful editing from time to time.

Sometimes we just lie to spare someone else's feelings, maybe by telling them they look great or that we really enjoyed that one-woman show they did in the back of the library. We even lie to ourselves to make ourselves feel better. I tell myself I look good, that no one will notice my double chin or that the scale is wrong and my hair is long.

A majority of the lies people tell are harmless. I read a report that most of our lies are small adjustments to the truth, like how much we paid for the hotel or how much money we made. I truly don't care what you spent on that new car, but if it makes you feel more comfortable by shaving a hundred dollars off, have at it. We're all storytellers.

The big lies are obviously repellent and way too hurtful. If a lie involves damaging spouses, business partners and other complicated relationships that survive on the honesty of all parties, it should not be told. Lies can literally destroy lives, so it's best to keep them at the level of complimenting someone's haircut when they really look like a rooster in a windstorm.

These are all basic parameters of lying, and forgive me if I have gone on too long but I just want to set up the kind of liar that really bothers me. You can tell me you're almost here, tell me your phone has been acting weird or that you didn't see my email. I can handle it. But don't you dare tell me that you were late because, while you were changing a flat tire, you had to fight off a biker gang with nothing but a tire iron and a lug nut.

That's just insulting. What these people are actually saying is that they think we're dumb enough to believe it. Ed did this nonstop. He told me that he boxed with Tyson, he ran with the bulls and he grabbed the blade of a helicopter and forced it to land.

He was a liar. He lied and lied and lied some more. Hardly anything truthful came out of this guy's weirdly shaped lips. Which is why when he told me the following story there was no way I could believe it, and, son of a bitch, I think it might have been true.

This strange pothead who was addicted to weed because his mom/girlfriend gave it to him ended up in a pretty bad spot after college. While most people graduated and moved on or went back to where they came from, Ed was lost. There were problems at home and he hadn't thought about what to do next, so he just stuck around the school. He was in a postgraduate purgatory and quickly ran out of money and ended up working in a children's shoe store at the mall, fitting young squirmy kids into shoes they didn't want.

This gave him a paycheck while he tried to figure out his life, but it also gave him a good view of the sporting goods store across the mall. He would watch when they came and went, and he realized that the security firm picked up the big bags of cash every Thursday just before closing time. So Ed, who told us that before he came to Rider College he had gotten an undergraduate nuclear physics degree from Princeton that was so top secret he was the only one who knew about it, figured Wednesday was the best day to break in and steal all the money.

He stayed late one Wednesday and offered to close up, which they must have been happy to let him do. I can only imagine the stories he must have told his fellow shoe salesmen when things got slow around the old shoe shop. So when he announced on this Wednesday night that his coworkers could go, they quickly went.

"And that's when I made my move," he said. "I quickly closed up our shop and jumped over to the sporting goods store. I could have run around the mall concourse, but I knew I didn't have that kind of time so I used my rock climbing abilities to climb off the banister, grab hold of the modern art display and propel myself to the other side like my trapeze training had taught me."

After he landed in front of the sporting goods store, he offered the pretty young lady a hand in closing up. She was always flirting with him down by the Jamba Juice, so he knew all he had to do was flirt while she was closing things down and he would be able to finagle the keys without her knowing it in a dazzling sleight of hand, the method of which was taught to him by Houdini's great-great-grandson, who had come in to buy some shoes.

"Once the gate was closed and I had the keys, I told her to wait for me in my car, and she just about took her panties off at the mention of spending some time together. She said I looked like a young Kevin Costner and ran off as I unlocked the gate, slid underneath like a ninja, kicked the security cameras with a high-velocity spin kick and was standing before the safe in a matter of seconds. That's when things got tricky."

He'd thought he remembered the code, but in a mathematical mix-up he had combined the safe combination with a new equation he was working on based on the Pythagorean Theorem.

"And wouldn't you know it: I put a two inside of a three, and that triggered not only their alarm system but the entire alarm system in the state, which had county and local cops swarming the place in a matter of minutes. So I did what my military training had taught me—I hid in a tent."

Another lie. He had no military training. He was our age, and even if he had taken a top-secret summer class at Princeton, it would still have left him with no time to even fill out a form for the military. He swore that it was not only his marine training that gave him the idea but that most of his knowledge about warfare came from the movie *Rambo*. He had not only seen it, he had consulted on the script (he would have been six), so he knew that as long as he could find a bowie knife and a satchel of beef jerky he would be walking out of this store with not only a big bag full of money but his honor.

"So the police show up and I know that there's only one thing cops hate more than trouble and that's disco music. So I hurled my bowie knife out of the back window of my tent, hit the play button on a boom box by the register and wouldn't you know it, there was a Bee Gees tape ready to go."

Apparently, when the police heard "Jive Talkin'," they were so angry that they called the whole thing off. "As soon as they cleared the store, I slid down the air duct, and landed right in the driver's seat of my car. The cops gave me a look like they couldn't believe it, so I reached into my money bag, gave them a twenty and told them to keep the change."

And here's where it gets weird. He doesn't get away. He just ends the story with "And then they arrested me." And here's the weirder part: He was arrested. He did go to jail. Our friend Dave visited him. And he was fired from the shoe store. There was an article in the paper that there had indeed been a lot of police presence at the mall. That someone had tried to rob the sporting goods store. They didn't name him, but everything else checked out.

Now that I think of it, though, he might have seen the story too and made it his own. Maybe he was in jail because he borrowed his mom's car, got pulled over for speeding and when he reached for his registration card the officer saw some weed in the glove box. Or maybe that woman was never his real mom to begin with.

DON'T FEAR THE CLOUD

....

My friend Dave has been moping around for so long he's starting to look like a basset hound. Everything on him has collapsed under the weight of living, and he doesn't contend with anything greater than what any of us deals with: annoying bills, a leaky sink, an uneven haircut, the usual humdrum of it all. But he thinks he has it harder than everybody else and walks around like a sad-eared donkey lost in the snow.

I can feel him approaching with the same rumbling energy of a summer thunderstorm. The sky darkens, the air changes, he walks in and just unloads, filling the room with a downpour of sad stories. He shares way too much and lately loves to talk in great detail about his hemorrhoid problem. He calls them the 'roids, as if they're annoying old college buddies who came for a visit and won't leave.

"I was stuck on the 101 for hours. The 'roids were screaming something fierce. I got one of those donut pillows you put under your ass, but after an hour in traffic even that didn't help. The 'roids were throbbing so bad I could feel it in my teeth."

I'll try to change the subject by bringing up something fun, like an upcoming game or a show we should go to.

"I can't say either way. There's no telling what kind of mood the 'roids will be in. It's going to have to be a game-time decision."

The exhausting part of being around him is the nonstop cheerleading I have to do. I've got to pull out my pom-poms and root him on at every turn, trying to show him that things aren't so bad, but sometimes that's tough to do because in his life, a lot of the time, things aren't so great. I don't know if it's bad luck or bad karma, but I have to believe he's somewhat responsible for turning the universe against himself.

He's just one of those guys. If we order food for delivery, his order will be wrong. If we go out to a restaurant, his dish will have a hair in it. If he tries to cook something at home, he will light his face on fire. It's happened.

He was frying up some Steak-umms, which are thin frozen cheese steaks, popular in places like college dorm rooms and the entire state of New Jersey. I'm not sure what they're made of, but the word "steak" is definitely misleading. All you have to do is toss a couple of them in a pan and heat them up. They're especially good at the end of a long drunken night when you've run out of money and sense. Dave, however, was sober when he tossed way too much oil into the pan, let it heat up to a zillion degrees and tossed in the frozen beef. Everything sizzled, popped and exploded like the grease fire it was. He tried to cover it with a dish towel, which also caught fire, and before he got it to the sink to douse it, he burnt off his eyebrows.

Seeing a friend without eyebrows is pretty confusing. There's something going on but you're not sure what, and for some reason your brain won't even consider the possibility. I thought that maybe he was missing a mustache, that maybe he'd gotten a haircut or that maybe he'd started wearing makeup.

"There's something different about you."

"There's never anything different about me."

"Something on your face . . . or missing from your face. Wait! What happened to your eyebrows?"

"I don't know what you're talking about."

And he didn't. He had no idea, until I pointed it out, that he had completely singed off both his eyebrows. He nonchalantly shrugged his shoulders and raised the skin where his brows should have been.

"Sounds about right."

It was just another day in the world of Dave.

Back when I heard he had a girlfriend, I thought this was finally his shot at improving his life. Sometimes we just need someone else around to pay close attention to us and point out our flaws in order to gently nudge us forward. But this doesn't work out so well if your partner is scarier than you are.

Jeni with an *i* didn't look particularly frightening. She dressed in conservative sweaters with little knitted flowers on them, straight practical pants and boring flat shoes. But what she was hiding under her librarian cover was a young woman who loved to fight.

Some people, particularly if they were raised by parents who constantly fought, love to have a partner they can use as a punching bag. They don't process fighting the way most people do; they actually enjoy it, and when Jeni found Dave she had found her punching bag.

For the first time he had a sexual partner, and he was more

than happy to give us the updates on all the crazy things she liked to do. Without going into too much detail, it's probably enough to say she was very inventive and extremely passionate, and Dave, who was a rookie in all departments, was at her mercy.

This had to be what kept him in the relationship, because there was no other reason to stay in something that caused him so much pain. She was constantly starting fights by attacking him for everything he did. She would attack him if he came home early, late or right on time. She just wanted to get out of that horrible blissful state into that comfort zone of ripping each other's heads off.

Dave would come over and sit on my couch looking like a fighter in his corner of the boxing ring who'd gotten punched repeatedly in the face. He was often dazed, stunned and confused, trying to make sense of what was happening to his world. Granted, his world was a somber place, but for the most part it was dull. Now he'd been thrust into the chaos of a prizefight, trying to keep his wits about him with blood in his eyes and a slight concussion.

As his corner man, I kept telling him to leave. He was a lot of things, but he wasn't a fighter; he simply didn't care enough. I felt if he stayed in the ring any longer he might not survive. But he wouldn't let me throw in the towel, because he was convinced that if he left the ring he would never have sex again.

The problem with helping a friend get out of a toxic relationship is that it doesn't happen quickly. There are many mini-breakups before it finally sticks, and sometimes it doesn't stick at all and your friend ends up breaking up with you instead. These are the risks you take, but if you love him it's worth the shot.

Eventually, when she thought he was cheating on her and lit his bed on fire, he literally saw the light. You should never say "I told you so," but I did, and it helped restore him back to his mopey self as he went to sleep safely on my couch.

While it was nice having the old Dave back, it wasn't long before I was pulling out my pom-poms again. I tried to cheer him up by taking him to the beach. I could say "We went to the beach," but more accurately, I took him, like a parent trying to cheer up his troubled teen by taking him on a trip, as if a change of scenery is all that's needed to stop the kid from hating everything and everybody, especially his parents.

When I picked him up at his apartment, he was sitting on the curb in the hot sun like an angry skate rat who'd just gotten kicked out of the 7–Eleven. When I think "beach," I think light colors, maybe a fun baseball cap or one of those country-fishing hats that old men wear but that are cool now because they come in fun bright colors with pineapples on them. You grab a T-shirt with Bob Marley on it or the logo of a discontinued soda brand from the seventies when companies got you to like them by selling "happy." Dave was dressed in all black like he was going to a Metallica concert: tight black jeans, black T-shirt and black boots.

You would have thought I was picking him up to take him to school. He pulled up his wool socks and sauntered to the car like he had fifty-pound weights on his back, dragging his Frankenstein feet as he went.

"Hey, you ready for the beach?"

"Whatever."

"Beautiful day. Did you forget your sunglasses?"

"They broke."

"Did you bring a change of clothes? A bathing suit? A towel?"

"No."

"Great. Let's hit it."

When we pulled into the parking lot, he said he was going to wait in the car but I wouldn't let him, explaining that it's illegal to leave vampires in a car during a heat wave. I made him carry a beach chair.

I've seen a lot of things at the beach—seagulls, cranes, pelicans—but I have never seen a black crow. That is, until I looked over at Dave and saw three giant black crows gathered around him like he was their leader. Two were in front of him as if they were waiting for an assignment and the third was perched on the back of his beach chair, making it look like it was sitting on his shoulder.

It was a little scary that he was so morose and troubled that these graveyard birds were attracted to his energy in what was an otherwise sunny, fun-filled beach scene. While children were building sandcastles and families were relaxing under brightly colored umbrellas, he sat there surrounded by black crows, rearranging himself in his seat to make room for the 'roids, like a vacationing Edgar Allan Poe.

It was the first time I'd seen him smile in a long while.

He needed me for a while, and I was happy to serve. He eventually found a normal girl and got married. His children are a delight. His wife is a ray of sunshine and he's *her* job now. He doesn't seem any happier, but now I can see that that's okay.

He's just a vehicle that runs in a different gear. You can't expect a tractor to run as hot and fast as a Ferrari and we shouldn't want it to. The world needs tractors, 'roids and all.

THAT'S AMORE

....

Occasionally, the athlete in me, who really has not done anything of note since I retired from high school football in 1986, will seek assistance on how to lose weight without having to move. I have come to terms with the fact that I no longer have knees healthy enough to climb even a flight of stairs without popping, disconnecting and nearly breaking. I think of my younger self, who had the ability to jump from the top of a six-foot fence without spraining his ankle, in the same way I reminisce about a loved one I have long since lost.

I can still safely participate in low-impact exercise activities, like swimming, or cycling, or senior citizen mall walking, but the amount of effort I truly exert wouldn't burn any more calories than one would find in a single Girl Scout Cookie. If I have any chance of losing weight or at least slowing how big and round I get, it all comes down to diet.

There is no end to the number of people in my life willing

to give me advice based on what they eat, what they have heard and what they have tried. And to all these well-meaning people who thought I was sincerely listening to them, I am sorry.

I'm sorry to my pal Joe, who talked to me for hours about adopting the keto diet. The keto diet is when you eat nothing but fatty Buffalo wings, bacon and Slim Jims in an attempt to teach your body to burn and function on nothing but fat. Before long your body is using fat for energy and your chubby breasts fall away like a discarded bra. It sounded fun at first, but it quickly grew tedious, and it turns out that while my body loves fat it also really wants potato chips and sourdough bread to dip in that fat.

I would like to apologize to my friend Rob, who convinced me several times that I should go vegan. I really liked the extreme nature of swearing things off for good. No meat. No drinking. No phone. It's clean, authoritative and strong. I actually lived that way for over a year, but eventually I found myself exhausted, and between two sold-out shows in Cleveland ate three baskets of French fries to keep me going. All it took was someone else telling me that my body needed more protein and I bailed. I tend to agree with whomever I speak to last.

I would like to apologize to my wife as well. She's a vegetarian, and although she wanted to leave me during my keto phase, she waited patiently for it to pass and then convinced me to shift to a plant-based diet. This idea was very appealing, because I knew it was filled with loopholes. Merely saying I was plant-based rather than plant-exclusive meant that I could freely leap into a crazy night of Korean barbecue or order a bacon cheeseburger while counting the fries as a plant.

I went off sugar for an afternoon, stopped drinking alcohol for a month and cut out all processed foods whenever I was somewhere other than an airport. I failed at all of these efforts, but at the risk of seeming weak I am going to use the childish excuse that I'm not to blame.

The first reason I fail at curbing my diet is that I'm a fat guy at heart. This is my natural state of being. I try to stay fit and eat the right things as much as I can, but the fat guy inside me is always doing something clever like sneaking Oreos into the shopping cart and ordering Pizza Hut when I'm not looking. He doesn't win all the time, but he's successful enough that I now carry two porterhouse-sized love handles on my sides.

Second, I'm Italian. That means that I love, appreciate and am literally made of great food. I have tomato sauce in my blood, skin made of prosciutto and a brain swimming in buffalo mozzarella. I was fed red wine in my bottle and raised in the kitchens of nonnas and nanas. And although I consider myself a decent Italian cook, when I'm lazy or simply looking for a safe harbor away from home I know that I will be loved and well fed in an Italian restaurant.

To be clear, we're not talking about Italy. There are a number of airlines that will fly you into that gorgeous country whose every city is filled with glorious restaurants, but I'm talking about America. This is where we find the Italian-American restaurant that took all the culinary styles of Italy and mixed them in a big bowl of Americana.

The real mark of a good Italian restaurant is a signed photo on the wall from Frank Sinatra. Sinatra is the George Washington of Italian-Americans, and if there was proof that he ate there, slept there or punched some guy in the mouth there, you were made.

The fewer number of tables the better. The really good spots have so few tables you need to make a reservation weeks or months in advance. Rao's in New York has ten tables. Il Mulino has maybe twelve and doesn't even have a sign on the building.

The Olive Garden has a million tables and anyone with a pair of Crocs and a credit card can get in.

I like a nice accordion. The accordion takes on different sounds in different places. Put it in New Orleans and you want to stuff your face with crawdads and stomp around to zydeco. You hear an accordion in Paris and you get a seat that faces the door with the hope of catching a glimpse of the spirit of Edith Piaf, who might take you back to her apartment, where together you'll float away to Bordeaux.

But the Italian accordion whips up images of red-and-white-checkered tablecloths, wine bottles encased in straw and a waitress who looks like all your aunts combined. Louis Prima is working the bar, Dean Martin is waiting tables and Martin Scorsese is telling jokes at the bar.

They're open all year: during the promising spring, the height of summer, the comforting fall—but I'll take the winter. The cold, hard winter that forces you to look for the warmth of a friendly garlic-coated cave. There will be focaccia and prosciutto and Parmesan crumbled off the block. There will be wine. Glorious wine. There will be fine wine, but the house wine can be even finer. There will be pepperoni, peppers, provolone and more. There's always more. More olive oil on the table, more bread, more laughs.

New York Italian restaurants were my training ground. My father would take us to Guido's in the Supreme Macaroni Co. in the shadow of the Port Authority on Ninth Avenue, made somewhat famous when Billy Joel featured it on the back of his album *The Stranger.*

We'd drive in from New Jersey, park on the street (never in a garage), and enter through an active pasta shop up front with large bins of dried pasta and giant bags of flour lining the walls.

Beyond the shop, through an open door, we entered into the classic Guido's.

The walls were covered with photos of past generations: stoic immigrant couples, serious young brides and children who for some reason were always on the backs of ponies. There was a cat who roamed the dining room, looking for scraps and a friendly leg to rub up against as friendly women dropped off plates of mussels and baked clams.

As I got older, I started to use it as my home base to get together with friends from high school as we reconnected after our college years. We'd meet near the holidays and gather around the table eating, drinking and laughing as we tried to anchor ourselves in our emerging adult lives over giant plates of meatballs and chicken Parmesan. It's a tradition that continues to this day, forged by the familial magic of a place that helped us to see that what we had as teenagers was deeper and better than what we found once we got older.

Another mainstay was Puglia's, on Hester Street in Little Italy. Surrounded by other Italian restaurants, Puglia's stood out mainly for its entertainment, which was comprised of a one-man phenomenon named Jorge Boccio. He looked like an aging Elvis, with big doo-wop hair and a giant diamond-studded "Jorge" belt buckle that completed his black, sparkly outfit, and would stand quietly at his keyboard, which was wedged in among the tables, barely noticed by the patrons.

In my early twenties I took a date there, without telling her what was going to happen. Expecting a romantic meal, she grew concerned when we were seated alongside strangers at a long picnic-style table. A boisterous waiter feigned taking our order while really telling us what we were going to eat. When my date tried to express her dietary restrictions, he rolled his eyes and laughed.

As we nibbled on some bread and got our drinks, I saw Jorge making his way behind his organ. People who knew what was about to happen, myself included, started to buzz. Jorge hit his first notes, said hello and started to play "That's Amore." I was smiling from ear to ear. My date was frightened.

"What is happening?" she asked.

"It's Jorge! Isn't he great?"

She started to look for the exit.

When Italians are trying to be quiet, they are emotional, expressive and loud. When they're given permission to let themselves go, they lose their minds, and Jorge was about to do just that. On the first notes of "Faniculi, Fanicula," people started singing along. When he rolled into "Mambo Italiano," some began dancing in the aisle. But when he broke into "The Napkin Song," what had been a restaurant quickly transformed into a family dining room at the holidays.

With practiced confidence, Jorge glided across the keyboard like a puppet master who was about to shake everyone to life. In a frenzy, everyone stood and started twirling their white cloth napkins in the air, pounding on the tables and screaming along. It was, as always at Puglia's, a great big Italian shit show.

As the music ended, everyone returned to normal and returned to their seats, elated, winded and a little friendlier toward their tablemates. This is what made Puglia's a family favorite, and if my date thought it was uncool and ridiculous, she never got invited back to that or any other place with me ever again.

The list of classics goes on and on: Monte's, Carmine's, Umberto's Clam House and Marinella. And as people lament the shrinking of New York's Little Italy to something even littler, new spots are opening all the time.

My newest tradition is marathon meals with the great comedian/rockstar Dave Hill at Gene's on West Eleventh Street, another red-sauce classic that has been around since 1919.

After a casual conversation revealed that Dave and I had both secretly loved this forgotten spot, with its dated décor, sleepy atmosphere and even sleepier clientele, we joined forces like members of a secret club and started meeting at the bar, which sits about eight people, tucked into the corner, once you come down the stairs.

The bartender is always happy to see us, because he knows we'll be eating, and he instantly transforms our spot with the small but dramatic placement of an open cloth napkin. Unlike at Puglia's, it will remain on the bar, where the cutlery is placed, the ice-cold martinis shaken and poured and the meal quickly begun with plates of bruschetta: chopped tomatoes, garlic, olive oil and basil atop small slices of bread. We didn't order the bruschetta, but at Gene's they start feeding you as soon as you sit down, just like a good Italian grandmother would.

Bruschetta is a good way to warm up, like stretching before you run, and gives us time to order a second martini before we move on to red wine, garlic bread and Dave's forbidden pleasure: plates of liver pâté. As the conversation crackles and we make grand plans for the future of comedy, the magic of Gene's sweeps over us and gives us a sense of belonging, just as it has for other New Yorkers for over a century.

As the night goes on and eventually dumps us back onto the street under the watchful streetlights, we return to our lives, happier and fatter than when we came in. That's why we always return, and why I will never be as skinny as I'd like to be.

PACK YOUR BAGS

We are seekers. We long for exploration and new experiences and what lies beyond the strip mall on the distant horizon. Unfortunately, the first step in any journey is a trip to the airport, which is at the very least annoying, extremely uncomfortable and most likely terrifying.

There are very few places where everybody is on edge. Anxious people with frayed nerves are trying to pretend that everything is normal when everybody knows they can lose it at any point. This, by the way, is why I am supporting babies who cry on airplanes. I know they're not a popular group, but it's time to join Team Baby. I'm always next to some businessman complaining about a crying infant.

"Will someone shut that damn kid up?"

No. You shut up. You're a man. A grown man with hairy arms and a wallet. You chose to be on this flight. That kid doesn't want to be here. A baby doesn't want to be on a plane at thirty thousand feet with its skeleton collapsing from the air pressure like a plastic Poland Spring bottle. He doesn't want to be sitting at ass level with a planeful of middle-aged gasbags crop-dusting him on their way to their seats.

No, this kid is in a horrible situation. He should be crying on the airplane. Actually, we should all be crying on the airplane. But of course we're too embarrassed, so we just mutter prayers into our Bloody Marys at six in the morning hoping we'll survive this death trip and see our loved ones again.

Now, if you want to complain about toddlers who have their own seats in business class, I'll listen to you, because that should be illegal. I count on those frequent-flier upgrades as I zigzag across the country. I was recently denied, and when I got on the plane I saw two toddlers sitting in my seats. That's tough to take. I'm trying to stay optimistic, and these kids are beating me at life. I know it's not their money, but they've got connections and they're working it. Now I'm stuck in the middle seat in coach between two dinosaurs while a toddler is standing naked on my seat drinking a mimosa and giving me the finger through the curtain.

I understand being frustrated and angry when you travel, because it's scary out there. That's why we like being at home. Home is safe. Home gives you the illusion that you have control over the universe, which of course you do not, but at least you know where the spoons are and where you keep the extra toilet paper.

But once you leave your home and go out into the world, you have very little control. You have been snatched out of your everyday life, where most everything has been figured out, and propelled into an adventure of nonstop challenges.

As soon as you get on the line at security, you are in trouble. You think you're doing everything right, when suddenly the TSA agent holds up your bag. Whose bag is this? Uh-oh.

"It's my bag."

"Is there an iPad in here?"

"Maybe."

"You're a moron."

"No, I'm a dad. I do things."

"No iPads, people. All electronics have to be removed from your bag and put in a bin. If you're wondering why the line is so long, you can thank old four-eyes here, who thinks he doesn't have to follow the rules."

From that point on you are faced with decision after decision. Even the hotel, your final destination, is filled with nonstop questions. How does the elevator work? How does the shower turn on? Why isn't it getting hotter? How does the remote control work? Where is the thermostat? Whose curly hair is this?

And how do you turn on the damn lamp? Why is every lamp different and where is the switch? Is it on the base, under the lampshade, on the side? Where is the damn switch? You put it on the wire? Underneath the end table? You heartless sons of bitches.

And this is the easiest travel you can have. Traveling alone with your wheelie bag. If you decide to travel with your family on a family vacation, you will be challenged in ways that you can't even imagine.

A family isn't a great organization to begin with. If you were building a company, would you give lifelong positions to everyone without a single interview? Never. Well, that's what a family is. It barely functions at home, so why would you take it out on the road?

And despite repeated disasters, I still hold out a naïve optimism that this time it will work out. I tell myself that all we have to do is get to the resort and then I can relax. Sure, the travel part will be hellish, but once we check in I will have time for myself. No. This never happens. Because now I have entered one of those torturous reality shows where I will be faced with the most insane challenges ever imagined.

Problems are hurled at you with breakneck speed.

"Your wife was bit on the ass by a jellyfish—go!"

"Your daughter threw her flip-flops out of the hotel window to the balcony below."

"Your wife fell asleep in the sun and is now covered in blisters."

"Your mother-in-law is trying out her new Spanish and saying slightly racist comments to the busboy."

"It's two o'clock in the morning, your youngest just broke out in hives and there's not a hospital within hours. What are you going to do?"

What am I going to do? I'm going to dig up an old Benadryl from my backpack, take the hair off it, give it to her, put her back in bed and hope she wakes up in the morning. I'm not a doctor, I'm a drunk dad on vacation.

And news flash: The kids don't want to be there either. Kids don't want to be trapped in a hotel room with their parents—the only two people who can get them in trouble. Our entire childhoods are spent getting away from our parents. We camp out in tree houses, sleep at our friends' houses and hide in piles of leaves. My friends and I used to play in a drainpipe. A pipe that took all the human waste from the town and dumped it into a lake. That's where we played, in the town shit pipe. And we loved it.

We loved it in that pipe. Because we knew our parents wouldn't look for us in there.

"Tommy's been gone all day. Where can they be?"

"Do you think they're in the shit pipe?"

"No, not my Tommy."

Yes. That's exactly where I was. Forget Disney—this was the happiest place on earth. I would much rather be in the shit pipe than in a hotel room with my half-naked parents.

THE FINAL OUT

....

I'm a big baseball fan, mainly for the conversation. Baseball is a game that gives the players and fans room to breathe, and from that room come some great debates and colorful conversations. The main voice, of course, comes from the broadcasters. The announcers in the booth are such an important part of the game that they can be nominated into the Baseball Hall of Fame alongside the greatest athletes.

But some of the freewheeling announcers from the past didn't age so well. For instance, retired announcer Ray "The Mouth" Criner, who was pushed out of the professional broadcast booth last year due to excessive profanity. His love for America's pastime wouldn't let him quit, so he started "Bleacher Bum," his own baseball podcast, which covers his eight-year-old grandson's Pee Wee League. The following was transcribed from his final broadcast from the Ty Cobb Memorial Ballpark in Bayonne, New Jersey.

"Well, sports fans, here we are, three outs away from the end of a truly horrible season, and it's about time somebody comes out and says it—this team stinks! All the hopefulness that the Liberty Bank Badgers had in early spring has gone down the crapper, leaving us with a collection of third graders who would have trouble winning if the other team skipped the game and canoed down the Delaware.

"While they trail the Jiffy Lube Cougars 12–0, it's only fitting that a thick, suffocating humidity has blanketed the field. It's so hot that a family of squirrels is playing in the Gatorade bucket like it's a water park, the few remaining fans in the stands are drenched in sweat like a pile of wet socks and Kyle's grandmother, also known as my wife, has locked herself in the air-conditioned car and refuses to get out. Well, keep the engine running, honey, this game is almost over, and we can thank the baseball gods for that.

"Back to the action. I couldn't think of a better kid to lead off this final inning for the Badgers than Brian "Boom-Boom" Bernstein. On draft day this kid was the talk of the league, showing real talent in the field and an uncanny ability to tie his cleats all by himself. But as luck would have it, Brian was hit with an accelerated growth spurt that has left him with the coordination of a newborn baby giraffe. He hasn't had a hit all season, and his aim is so bad I can only imagine what his mother has to clean up in the family commode.

"Here comes the pitch, Brian looks the other way and swings, hits himself in the leg with the bat and takes strike one. You know, this happened to a cousin of mine: He grew so much over the summer that he started tripping on his own hands and grew an Adam's apple that was so big it won a ribbon at the state fair. Here comes the pitch, and it's in there for strike two.

"Boom-Boom has had a terrible year, but now he seems kind of happy up there, as if he's sensing the end. I had that same goofy feeling when the missus wheeled me to the car after my last colonoscopy, and I'm happy to report I was clean as a whistle.

"Here's the windup and the pitch, and it's strike three. He's out, and is jumping for joy—he's dropped his bat, tossed his cap and is literally skipping to the parking lot. Well, there he goes, and I doubt this town will see the likes of Boom-Boom in a baseball uniform ever again. Hey, Brian, give cheerleading a try. I hear dudes do that now.

"Well, two more outs and we can all get out of here and still make the happy-hour specials at Applebee's. Not that these kids need any more food. Before the game even starts, the parents are drowning the kids in spicy tuna hand rolls and chicken parm sandwiches. Back in my day you played hard in hopes that if you won you might be rewarded with a sip from a rusty water fountain.

"Next up is Kelly Peterson, who's back from a three-game suspension after biting her first base coach. Say what you will about the small fry, but this kid's got spirit. She may be no taller than a box of crackers, but tucked in that tiny package is one of the fiercest third graders I've ever seen.

"She digs in and here comes the pitch and, oh, she fouls it off. She actually got a piece of that one, which is practically a home run for this ball club. You know, it really makes you wonder if she'll always be short. If her father is any indication, she may be destined for Smallville. He's a little fella and plenty angry about it, always barking like a terrier at the other parents in the bleachers, and in my opinion he's lucky he doesn't get a punch in the nose. Back in my day a pip-squeak knew his place.

"Here comes the pitch—she swings and misses. She didn't

like that at all, and now she's giving the pitcher the finger. You don't like to see that, but again, I do like her spunk. Uh-oh, now Kelly is giving the finger to everyone in the stands. This is getting ugly, and it looks like the ump . . . yup, the umpire, fourteen-year-old Justin Smith, just threw her out of the game, and now Kelly is biting him on the leg. She's locked on like a pit bull on a raw steak smothered in A.1. Now a group of parents are pulling her off, the ump is crying and it's total chaos.

"This is a good time to let you know that our sponsor, the good people at bigenvelopes.com, want to make mailing easier than ever. That's bigenvelopes.com, because going to the post office is a pain in the ass.

"All right, things seem to have calmed down, and while that was crude and rude, this may have been the best thing to happen to the Badgers in a long time. Definitely the funniest. So we're down to the final out, and hopefully they won't get on base because I can see that my wife has fallen asleep and I'm starting to wonder if she actually turned the car on. Well, hopefully she left the window open a crack or it's going to be one weird party after the game.

"Any-hoo, coming up to bat is none other than my grandson, Kyle 'The Crybaby' Kowalski. That's not me being mean, folks, them's just the facts. Love him to death, but this kid cries as soon as he opens his eyes. There's been a lot of internet searches and family discussions, but if you ask me the kid is just plain soft and his father is to blame.

"Kyle digs in, here comes the pitch and it's low and outside—ball one. His dad means well, but he overcompensates for all his time traveling away from home, and by the way he showers the kid with gifts it makes you wonder how many gals he's got out there on the road. Back in my day if your dad bought you a surprise comic book there was a good chance that in nine months you'd be surprised with a new brother in another town. Now, that was something to cry about.

"Here comes another pitch and, Holy Toledo, Kyle actually hit the ball and it's rolling all the way to the fence! Kyle is rounding first and is on his way to second base. The outfielder tosses it to the cutoff man and Kyle is heading to third. The cutoff man turns and throws. It's going to be close. Kyle slides. He doesn't know how to slide. Here comes the throw, Kyle falls in a heap, short of the bag, here's the tag and . . . he's out. Kyle is out, the game is over and here come the waterworks.

"Well, that's it, folks, the Cougars are dancing around on the mound, the season is over and the Liberty Bank Badgers end with a record of zero and eight. Well, suck it up, Kyle, let's grab a tuna roll, head to the car and see if Grandma is still alive.

"This is Ray 'The Mouth' Criner wishing you a happy summer filled with baseball, big broads and a couple of beers."

REGRETS? I HAVE A BUNCH

....

I wish I could be one of those people who live without regrets. I've heard them in interviews and read their quotes. "I regret nothing. If I could do it all over I'd do it all exactly the same." Wow. They're either delusional, thoughtless or on really good meds.

You regret nothing? Really? How about that tattoo? How about eating tuna fish at the San Francisco airport before a red-eye flight? What about that girl you dated or that guy you married? How about that shirt you have on right now? Yeah, and all that other stuff you wore in all those pictures from every day before this one? Not to mention all the stuff you said. No regrets? That's unbelievable. As in, I do not believe you.

I don't go a single day without saying something I regret. Regrets are healthy. Regrets are constructive. If you have no regrets, then you haven't grown. If you cheat on your girlfriend and you break up and she is hurt, you should regret that. And what enables you to regret that is that you have evolved into a person who knows better and hopefully won't do that again.

I did some mean and devious things as a child. My friends and I rode our bikes past a blind man finding his way with his walking stick on the side of the road, and rather than help we yelled out and scared him half to death. Looking back over my shoulder and seeing his twisted face frozen in fear with his stick planted in the cement made me feel so horrible that I carry that feeling with me to this day. I regretted it, and knew immediately that I would never be that awful ever again.

I would love it if that was the only lesson I needed to learn, but unfortunately I had to learn other lessons over and over throughout childhood and into my teens. When we started to drive, we played this horrible trick on people. We would drive up alongside them and wave and point at the back of their car as if they were some sort of problem with their rear tire. We thought it was funny that we had the power to make someone pull over and get out of their car.

We did it all the time. Until the day we were driving on the Garden State Parkway, pulled up on this car filled with a family and started waving. One of the three children in the back saw us first and tapped the father on the shoulder. This man turned to us with the most expressive face I had ever seen.

He looked like a big old hound dog, with bouncy cheeks, a big lovable nose and the biggest, brownest eyes ever found on any person since the beginning of time. He didn't just look at us—he took us in, and mouthed a giant "thank you" for warning him about whatever trouble we'd found on his car.

What really killed me was that we had manipulated his trust. He trusted this group of loving boys who were going out of their way to help him. His eyes swelled with tears—grateful, trusting tears. But then he caught himself and grabbed the wheel tightly, because he had a job to do. He had to address this trouble that had put his family in danger. He needed to navigate to the side of this busy highway and change the tire or remove the debris or diffuse the bomb, whatever horrible thing these helpful Boy Scouts were warning him about.

As we pulled ahead and looked back at his slowing car, we didn't laugh. We let out a collective groan. A groan of regret for going out of our way to be shitty to someone just for a laugh over something that wasn't funny. And today I also regret that now I'm the guy with poor eyesight and fading skills driving along worrying about his family.

How can you have ever fallen out of love without having regretted the outcome? You enter into a relationship filled with hope and good intention, and suddenly one of you gives the other a knowing look and you both realize there won't be too many more dinners together.

I have a lot of minor regrets on almost a daily basis. I regret that I didn't say that thing to that person at just the right time. I regret that I didn't stay one day longer or get out of there one moment earlier.

If only I had invested in Apple when I was ten.

Did Lincoln regret going to the theater? Did MC Hammer regret that he wore those pants? I hope not.

Sometimes I do questionable things without any regret. I ate an entire bag of salt and vinegar potato chips yesterday while standing in line at the supermarket. I didn't plan on it. I wasn't trying to hurt anyone; I wasn't looking to eat the whole thing while standing up. But there I was pouring the remaining chip dust into the back of my throat while the cashier tried to figure out how she was going to scan it. I don't regret a damn thing about it and know without a doubt that I will do it again.

You don't want to be swallowed up by regrets. I have embraced my fair share of mistakes. I make mistakes all the time and let them go. I got on the wrong road and went the wrong way. What else is new?

I have eaten a lot of stupid things and gone to a lot of stupid places with a lot of stupid people. All mistakes, and I don't regret much of it.

Some things I feel like I'm supposed to regret but don't. I don't regret skipping wakes and funerals. Especially wakes. I went to one wake when I was a small child and stood in the room with a dead body at the other end and decided then and there that this wasn't right. I'm all for saying goodbye and visiting the survivors, but nobody needs to see their loved one in a box, dressed up like a ventriloquist dummy. Some people say this ritual provides closure, but so does never getting another phone call from them ever again.

I never regret going home early. I like going out. I like seeing people. I like doing things. But the joy that I have felt while walking into a concert, party or ball game is no match for the happiness of walking back out. I'm too worried about getting back to enjoy being away, so why even go away in the first place, and if I have to go then let's at least get back as quickly as we can.

I don't regret eating weird food and trying something new. If somebody eats something and they enjoy it, I'll give it a shot. Chinatown is filled with things that I would never have considered food, but if other people are eating it sign me up.

Love creates some regrets, but for the most part to love and be loved even for a little while is not regrettable. We met, we loved, we tried.

I did regret fooling around with Priscilla in seventh grade. She was Joe's girlfriend and everybody knew it but I liked her too. Joe saw us kissing outside the cafeteria and he didn't say anything. He didn't have to. We knew we were wrong, and after kissing that day and again that night and again the rest of the week we eventually started to kind of regret it, but at that age there are other forces at work in our bodies that far outweigh regret.

I guess we can allow for one loophole in the regret contract we make with ourselves. If we grow from the experience, then the person who did those things is no longer around. We are the better version of the individual who thought it was okay to act that way. So, if we have sincerely evolved, shouldn't we be allowed to toss our regrets away just like we tossed away that horrible zebra-striped shirt with the zippers? In a way we do, but we never really forget and that's okay.

All we can do is to try our best to live a good life. And you can't regret that.